KU-655-889

INTRODUCTION

To search for the ideal city today is useless. For all cities are different. Each one has its own spirit, its own problems, and its own pattern of life. As long as the city lives, these aspects continue to change. Thus to look for the ideal city is not only a waste of time but may be seriously detrimental. In fact, the concept is obsolete; there is no such thing.

– Steen Eiler Rasmussen (1898-)

Introduction

Welcome to SimCity 2000.

When you play SimCity 2000, you become the planner, designer and mayor of an unlimited number of cities. You can take over and run any of the included scenario cities, or build your own from the ground up.

You're in charge. You can choose to build small, rural towns, or huge bustling megalopolises. As you design and build your cities, simulated citizens, known as Sims, move in and build their homes, stores and workplaces, raise their families and invite their friends. If your city is a nice place to live, your population will increase. If it's not, your Sims will leave town. And be assured that they'll let you know what they think about you and your policies.

One of the toughest challenges of SimCity 2000 is to maintain a huge city without sacrificing your Sims' quality of life, without going broke maintaining the infrastructure, and without raising taxes so high that businesses relocate. SimCity 2000 lets you face the same dilemmas that mayors all over the world are facing. We've all said at one time or another that we could do a better job than our elected officials—here's your chance to prove it.

SimCity 2000 is primarily a "building" game, where you create and try to increase the size of your cities—but you also have plenty of opportunities to destroy. From bulldozers to earthquakes to air crashes, the implements of destruction are only a mouse-click away. But remember, it's a lot more challenging to build than to destroy, and the lives, hopes and dreams of millions of Sims are in your hands.

Credits

The Program
Designed By: Fred Haslam and Will Wright
Macintosh Programming: Fred Haslam, Will Wright, Justin McCormick, Mick Foley
IBM Programming: Jon Ross, Daniel Browning, James Turner
Windows Programming: James Turner, Jon Ross
Producer: Don Walters
Art Director: Jenny Martin
Computer Art: Suzie Greene (Lead Artist), Bonnie Borucki, Kelli Pearson, Eben Sorkin
Music: Sue Kasper, Brian Conrad, Justin McCormick
Sound Driver: Halestorm, Inc.
Sound Effects: Maxis Sample Heds, Halestorm, Inc.
Technical Director: Brian Conrad
Newspaper Articles: Debra Larson, Chris Weiss
Special Technical Assistance: Bruce Joffe (GIS Consultant), Craig Christenson (National Renewable Energy Laboratory), Ray Gatchalian (Oakland Fire Department), Diane L. Zahm (Florida Department of Law Enforcement)

The Manual
Written By: Michael Bremer
Copy Editors: Debra Larson, Tom Bentley
Documentation Design: Vera Jaye, Kristine Brogno
Documentation Layout: David Caggiano
Contributions To Documentation: Fred Haslam, Will Wright, Don Walters, Kathleen Robinson
Special Artistic Contributions: John "Bean" Hastings, Richard E. Bartlett, AIA, Margo Lockwood, Larry Wilson, David Caggiano, Tom Bentley, Barbara Pollak, Emily Friedman, Keith Ferrell, James Hewes, Joey Holliday, William Holliday

The Package
Package Design: Jamie Davison Design, Inc.
Package Illustration: David Schleinkofer

The Maxis Support Team
Lead Testers: Chris Weiss (Macintosh), Alan Barton (DOS)
QA: Alan Barton (Supervisor), Manny Granillo, Chris Weiss, Roger Johnsen, Don Horat
Tech Support: Carter Lipscomb (Manager), Kevin O'Hare, Peter Alau, Chris Blackwell, Kirk Lesser
Beta Testing: Robert McNamara, Steve Perrin, and all of Maxis
Product Manager: Larry Lee
Public Relations: Lois Tilles and Sally Vandershaf
Manufacturing: Val Garcia, Kim Vincent, Gina Martinez

Thanks To
Jeff Braun, Joe Scirica, Jim Siefert, Bob Derber, Sam Poole, Robin Harper, Michael Perry, Cassidy, Joell Jones, all the rest of the Maxoids who made this possible, and 'The Veddy Bad Girlfriend'

Contents

SIM CITY 2000
THE ULTIMATE CITY SIMULATOR

USER MANUAL
by Michael Bremer

On the whole I'd rather be in Philadelphia.
— W.C. Fields (1879-1946)

MAXIS

18/20 ST JOHN STREET

LONDON ECIM 4AY

TEL: 071 - 490 2333

FAX: 071 - 490 2177

Software copyright 1993 Sim-Business, Will Wright and Fred Haslam.
All rights reserved worldwide.
Manual copyright 1993, Sim-Business.
All rights reserved worldwide. No portion of this manual may be copied, reproduced, translated or reduced to any electronic medium or machine-readable form without the prior written consent of Sim-Business.

Maxis Software License Agreement
THE ENCLOSED SOFTWARE PROGRAMS ARE LICENSED BY MAXIS TO CUSTOMERS FOR THEIR NON-EXCLUSIVE USE ON A SINGLE COMPUTER SYSTEM PER THE TERMS SET FORTH BELOW.

License
You have the non-exclusive right to use the enclosed programs on a single computer. You may not electronically transfer the programs from one computer to another over a network. You may not distribute copies of the program or documentation to others. You may make one (1) copy of the program disks solely for backup purposes. If you install the program on a hard disk or other mass-storage device, a copy made of the program, as installed, as a part of, and solely for, archive purposes is also permitted. You may transfer the software from one computer to another on a permanent basis only, and only when all copies of the software on the original computer are removed on a permanent basis. YOU MAY NOT USE COPY, MODIFY, SUBLICENSE, RENT, LEASE, CONVEY, TRANSLATE, OR TRANSFER THE PROGRAMS OR DOCUMENTATION, OR ANY COPY EXCEPT AS EXPRESSLY PROVIDED IN THIS AGREEMENT. YOU MAY NOT CONVERT THE SOFTWARE TO ANY PROGRAMMING LANGUAGE OR FORMAT, DECOMPILE OR DISASSEMBLE THE SOFTWARE OR ANY COPY, MODIFICATION OR MERGED PORTION, IN WHOLE OR IN PART.

Limited Warranty
THESE PROGRAMS ARE PROVIDED "AS IS" WITHOUT WARRANTY OF ANY KIND EITHER EXPRESSED OR IMPLIED, INCLUDING BUT NOT LIMITED TO THE IMPLIED WARRANTIES OF MERCHANTABILITY AND FITNESS FOR A PARTICULAR PURPOSE. THE ENTIRE RISK AS TO THE RESULTS AND PERFORMANCE OF THE PROGRAMS ARE ASSUMED BY YOU. MAXIS DOES NOT WARRANT THAT THE FUNCTIONS CONTAINED IN THE PROGRAMS WILL MEET YOUR REQUIREMENTS OR THAT TH OPERATION OF THE PROGRAMS WILL BE UNINTERRUPTED OR ERROR FREE. The sole and exclusive remedy available to the purchaser or user of this software an accompanying documentation is a refund or replacement of the product, at the option of Maxis.

To the original purchaser only, Maxis warrants the magnetic diskette on which this software product is distributed. It is warranted to be free from defects in materials and faul workmanship under normal use for a period of ninety days from the date of purchase. If during this ninety-day period the diskette should become defective, it may be returned Maxis for a replacement without charge. The media warranty period is automatically extended upon receipt of the registration card.

Windows, Windows 3, Microsoft, and Microsoft Windows are registered trademarks of Microsoft Corporation.
IBM is a registered trademark of International Business Machines, Inc.
Macintosh and Apple are registered trademarks of Apple Computer, Inc.
Maxis and SimCity are registered trademarks and SimCity 2000 is a trademark of Sim-Business.

This manual is divided into four main sections:

The **Introduction** welcomes you to SimCity 2000, explains a little about the manual in general, helps you get the game up and running on your computer and sends you on your way to play.

The **Tutorials** are small guided tours through different aspects of city-building with SimCity 2000.

The **Reference** section describes in detail all the windows, buttons, features and functions of SimCity 2000, and explains much of the behind-the-scenes simulation action.

The **Gallery** section consists of contributions from a number of people to give you varying views, feelings, interpretations and predictions about real cities in words and pictures. Some of these individual pieces are located at the back of the manual in the "official" Gallery section. Others are spread throughout the rest of the manual.

And for those who are familiar with an earlier version of SimCity, there is an **Appendix** that lists SimCity 2000's new features and differences from the earlier versions.

In addition, the SimCity 2000 package includes a machine-specific Addendum to cover installation, startup, and any special features and functions on your computer.

SIM CITY 2000

From SimCity to SimCity 2000

If you're already familiar with an earlier version of SimCity, then you should have no trouble moving into SimCity 2000. If you haven't played SimCity before, then skip the rest of this section. You will not be quizzed on this material.

A few major features have changed and some tools have moved since the earlier versions of the game, so you may have just a little trouble finding things. A summary of all the changes and differences between the programs can be found in the Appendix. But to help you get started, here are the three most-asked questions by SimCity users when we sat them down in front of SimCity 2000:

- **Where the heck are the power plants?**
They're in a submenu under the power icon. Select Power Plant... from the submenu and you'll have a choice of from three to nine different power sources, depending on the city's date.

- **I click and click—why won't the durn thing set down zones?**
Instead of the fixed-size zones that you plop down, SimCity 2000 lets you make any size square or rectangular zone by clicking and dragging the mouse where you want to zone. You can zone over roads and rails, and place roads and rails in zones. By the way, airports and seaports are placed the same way as zones.

- **What's the deal with the water system?**
We've added a water system to the game, including pumps, pipes, treatment plants, water towers and desalinization plants. You don't need to worry about water to start a city. But you will need a water system before the population can grow very dense.

Getting Started

SimCity 2000 must be installed to a hard disk before it can be run. Please look in the machine-specific Addendum for complete instructions on installing SimCity 2000 to your hard disk and on starting the program.

Once you're up and running, feel free to jump right in and play, or if you want some guidance and a quick introduction to the main features and functions of the game, check out the tutorials.

TUTORIAL

The experts are all saying that our big cities have become ungovernable. What the hell do the experts know?
Newsweek, April 5, 1971

  – Richard J. Daley (Mayor, Chicago) (1902-1976)

Tutorials

Congratulations! By the virtue of owning SimCity 2000 you are hereby proclaimed Mayor of a million cities and ruler of a billion simulated lives (your Sims). It's a tough game, but somebody's gotta play it.

These tutorials are designed to help you adjust to your new office with as little transition time as possible.

There are three tutorials, each designed to be finished in one short sitting so you can get them out of the way and get on with the important business of building and running your cities. The first one is a general overview of the basic features of SimCity 2000—enough so you can start a new city, and get going on your own. The second one focuses on creating, editing and modifying your city's terrain, both before and after you've begun building your city. The third one goes into detail on a few of the advanced features.

We suggest that you whip through the first tutorial, then go play on your own for a while. You may figure everything else out on your own, and never need the other tutorials, but they're here if and when you want them.

This series of vignettes about cities and city planning was provided by Richard Bartlett, AIA, Architect. Spread throughout the manual, they give a historical and humanistic perspective to planning that you may wish to incorporate into your city designs.

Cities are for people: a place for their hopes and dreams, their work and play, their homes and homes for their children. Cities are alive and have personalities, each different from all others and each in constant change. A living organism made up of its collective inhabitants, a city is many things, but it is above all a storehouse of human characteristics.　I

Before jumping into the tutorials, take a moment to look over the following skills and conventions that will make your stay in SimCity 2000 a pleasant one.

SimCity 2000 requires a mouse. To play, you must know how to use a mouse for the following actions:

- Click—point the cursor to an object and briefly press the left (or only) mouse button.

- Double-click—point the cursor to an object and briefly press the left (or only) mouse button twice quickly.

- Click and drag—point the cursor to an object, then press and hold the left (or only) mouse button, then move the mouse to drag the object. Release the mouse button to release the object.

Unless otherwise specified, whenever this manual refers to clicking, double-clicking or clicking and dragging, use the left (or only) mouse button.

When you see the term "Shift-click," it means to hold down either Shift key on the keyboard and click the mouse button.

When you see the term "Option/Control-click," it means:

- On a Macintosh you should hold down the Option key on the keyboard while you click; or

- On a DOS or Windows-based computer you should hold down the Control key on the keyboard while you click.

SIM CITY 2000

Instructions and Explanations

In these tutorials, when you see text that looks like the text in this paragraph, it's an explanation of something.

When you see text that looks like this, it's an actual instruction for you to follow.

When you see text that looks like this, it's a note or a warning or other important message.

What Makes a [Sim]City?

To prepare you for building your city in the rest of this tutorial, here is a basic explanation of exactly what is city in SimCity 2000 is made of.

While SimCity has many layers of complexity and lots and lots of features and all sorts of stuff to put in your city, it's fairly easy to get a small city started. All you need is:

- A place for the Sims to live: a residential zone
- A place for the Sims to work: an industrial zone
- A place for the Sims to shop and conduct business: a commercial zone
- A source of power: a power plant
- A way to get the power from the power plant to the zones: power lines
- A way for Sims to travel between work, home or shops: roads

That's all you need to build, and Sims with that pioneering spirit will move into your city and build their own houses, factories and offices. They'll drive their cars and carry on business and complain about taxes. If you build it, they will simulate.

A small ring of stones holds together the glowing embers of last night's fire. Leaning on his staff, the herdsman quietly scans his flock, also contained within a larger circle of boulders and posts. Maximum land within minimum fence— today we call this radiocentric planning.

II

Once your city has begun to grow, you can add:

- More zones with different density levels
- Multiple above- and below-ground means of transportation
- A complete water system
- Custom landscaping
- Airports and seaports
- Police and fire stations
- Educational and recreational facilities
- A whole lot more

Enough talk ... time for a simulating experience.

In the distance an ox pulls against the farmer's timber plow, adding another straight line to an ever-widening rectangular plot of soil. As a time-saving invention, the plow gave the farmer freedom for other pursuits, but because it was a shaper of plots, it was the precursor of planning—zoning by brute force.

III

SIM CITY 2000

Tutorial 1— The Basics

The Start of Something Big

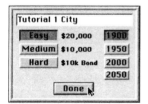

If you haven't already, take a look at your machine-specific Addendum, and install SimCity 2000 to your hard drive.

Start SimCity 2000.

See your Addendum for instructions.

Either the first time you play the game or during installation, you will be asked to enter your name to personalize your copy of SimCity 2000. Be sure to type your full name—and be polite because the name that you type in will appear a number of times and places in the game.

Soon a list of four choices will appear; it's time for your first real decision. Here you can load a city that you've already saved, start a brand-new city, edit a new map (we'll be doing this in Tutorial 2), or play one of the pre-built scenarios. For this tutorial, we'll want to start a new city.

Click on Start New City.

In mere moments you'll see a dialog box that asks you to make three decisions: how hard or easy you want your game to be, what year the game should start, and what your new city should be named. The defaults are Easy and 1900, which will be just fine, so all we need to do is type in the name.

Make sure the City Name is highlighted and type in: Tutorial 1 City.

Click on Done.

Note: On the Macintosh or other computers that allow long file names, the city name you type here will also be your file name. On computers that run DOS or Windows, where file names must be shorter, you'll get to type in a file name when you save the city to disk.

Soon the founding of your city will be announced in the newspaper. The newspaper is your tool for staying in touch with your adoring SimConstituents.

Click on the headline. Read the story that zooms out. Click again.

Open and read the other stories if you like, by clicking on them.

Click in the Close box in the upper-left corner of the Newspaper to send it to the recycling bin.

You are now looking at the City window, where you will spend most of your time as you build, run and rule your city.

A Window on Your City

At the top of the window is the Title bar. It contains the current city date, the city name, and the amount of money you have in your city treasury.

Over on the left side of the screen is the City toolbar. It has lots of buttons—your tools for creating and running your city.

Note: Every January, the Budget window will pop up. For now, just click on its Done button to make it go away. We'll worry about the budget later. If the Newspaper pops up, click on its close box.

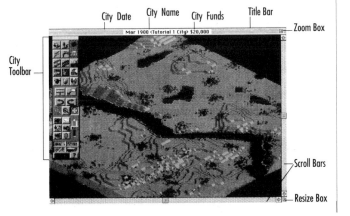

In the window itself you see the site of your city-to-be. A pristine wilderness: bare land, some forest areas and some flowing water. And the land isn't flat—there are hills and valleys, peaks and canyons. The terrain is divided into tiny squares. Each of these squares is called a "tile." Each tile is approximately one acre, or a 200 x 200 foot square.

We'll explore your new domain in a moment, but first, we need to take a detour and go straight to the top ... of your screen.

And on the Menu Tonight...

At the top of your screen is, of course, the Menu bar. These menus are well-behaved and work just like the menus in your other programs. Click and hold on the menu name to open the menu, slide the cursor to the menu item you want to activate, then release the mouse button.

Take a moment and open each of the menus, revealing their hidden glory.

Once you've looked them over:

Open the Options menu.

Select Auto-Budget.

This option makes the simulation repeat the same budget until you tell it otherwise—and stops that pesky Budget window from popping up and spoiling your view.

Open the Disasters menu.

Select No Disasters.

This setting keeps random disasters from occurring. (Those disasters really mess up a tutorial.)

For safety against roving thieves and predators, the farmer and herdsman laid their camps together, and through this simple act of survival and cooperation, attracted like-minded countrymen into their midst. The camp became a village, with a better standard of living, and more visitors became residents... and the village continued to grow.　　IV

And speaking of views, behold the vistas and valleys of your city-to-be. How'd you like another angle on the place?

Click on the Rotate Counter-Clockwise button in the City toolbar.

Do it again.

Click on the Rotate Clockwise button until you find the angle that pleases you.

As you can see, you can rotate the city and view it from all sides. This'll come in very handy later, when you're building your city. What's that? You want a closer view? No problem.

Click once on the Zoom In button in the City toolbar.

How's that? Closer?

Click again on the Zoom In button.

That's as close as you get. (Notice that the Zoom In button is ghosted and unavailable.) Now that you're here, how do you get around? Let's zoom out for a wider view, then do some travelin'.

Click once on the Zoom Out button.

Click on the Center button.

Click anywhere on the landscape.

The landscape will redraw in the City window, centered on the spot where you clicked. You can also use the Scroll bars to move around the landscape, but the Center button gives you more precise control.

A millennium would pass before any substantial innovations would drastically change the size or character of cities. But then...

"...within a very recent period, three new factors have been suddenly developed which promise to exert a powerful influence on the problems of city and country life. These are the trolley, the bicycle, and the telephone. It is impossible to foresee at present just what their influence is to be on the question of the distribution of population; but this much is certain, that it adds from five to fifteen miles to the radius of every large town. It is by such apparently unimportant, trifling, and inconspicuous forces that civilization is swayed and moulded in its evolutions and no man can foresee them or say whither they lead..." — F.J. Kinsbury, 1895

V

SIM CITY 2000

Make Yourself at Home

A nice, flat spot.

Let There Be Zones

A residental zone.

Time to pick a spot to found your city. Since each landscape generated by SimCity 2000 is different, the landscape on your screen, and therefore the city that you build, won't look exactly like the one in this manual—but it should be close. Kinda. Sorta. Maybe.

Click on the Zoom Out button until you are as far out as you can get.

Look for a nice, flat spot.

If there is water nearby, or even running through your spot, all the better, but not necessary. If there is no spot in your city that you are willing to call home, then open the File menu, and select New City. You'll be asked if you want to save the old one—click No. Then a new landscape will be generated, and you'll get to name your city and all that other stuff you did a few pages ago. You can repeat this until you find a home.

Once you're satisfied, then it's time to zone out.

As mentioned in What Makes a (Sim)City above, we'll need three kinds of zones in our city: residential, where the Sims live, commercial, for offices and stores, and industrial, for factories.

Survey your chosen territory and pick a spot to zone residential. If there is water nearby, include some waterfront in your zone.

Click on the Residential Zone button.

Click and drag on the landscape to form a rectangle where you want to make a residential zone.

You can zone right over hills and trees.

Now find a spot for the industrial zone. It is in your Sims' best interest to leave a bit of a buffer zone between residential and industrial zones.

Click on the Industrial Zone button.

Click and drag on the landscape to form a rectangle where you want to make an industrial zone.

Now find a spot for a commercial zone. Close to residential is handy. Some waterfront is nice, but not necessary.

Click on the Commercial Zone button.

Click and drag on the landscape to form a rectangle where you want to make a commercial zone.

Power to the People

The Sims that live in SimCities may have that pioneering spirit, but they won't move in until you supply electric power. After all, they *are* electronic life-forms.

To supply power, you need a power plant of some sort and power lines to get the power to where you want it. Both of these things are available from the Power button in the City toolbar.

Click and hold on the Power button in the City toolbar.

Move the cursor to highlight Power Plant... and release the mouse button.

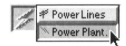

An assortment of power plants will appear, with pictures of, prices for and outputs from each plant. There is also an INFO button for each power plant that brings up even more fascinating facts. Power plants are not available to you until the city year reaches the time when that technology is available. In other words, you can't have nuclear fusion in 1901.

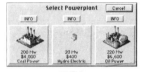

Click on the Coal Power Plant.

The power plant assortment will disappear, and a grey 4 x 4-tile shadow will follow the cursor. This is the size of the base of the power plant. Find a place—preferably near your industrial zone and far from your residential zone—to place the power plant. It must be placed on flat ground.

Click on the terrain to place your power plant.

Now we need to power up the zones. We'll need power lines to get the power from the power plant to each zone. Power won't travel from zone to zone without power lines, even if they're touching. Within zones, the building-to-building power lines are built by the Sims when they build their buildings. (But that's a private sector problem—you only have to power up each zone.)

I've Got a Line on You

Placing power lines can be a bit tricky, so it's best to zoom in as close as you can get.

Click on the Center button.

Click on your power plant.

Click on the Zoom In button until you are as close as you can get.

Click and hold on the Power button in the City toolbar.

Move the cursor to highlight Power Lines and release the mouse button.

You're ready to lay some power lines.

Click or click and drag to place power lines that connect the power plant to each of your zones.

If you place power lines that aren't connected to power, they'll blink to indicate that they aren't hooked up yet. If your power lines flash, then you've missed a connection. You may have to rotate the terrain to get a good look at your power plant from all sides.

Note: Laying power lines in hilly areas can be tricky. You may have to rotate the landscape and zoom in for a good close look. Try to stay on flat land for this tutorial.

Villages, cities, landscapes, regions and places in general derive their uniqueness from intangible forces. A sensitive planner or architect will recognize these qualities and incorporate them into the master plan.

VI

The Drive to Thrive

Now all we need is a transportation system, and your town should be ready for some Sims to move in.

Click on the Road button in the City toolbar.

Click and drag through and around your zones to set up a network of roads.

By the time you get your roads down, some Sims should be moving into your town.

Power cannot travel through roads without wires, so place power lines across the roads to make sure each section of every zone has power.

Click and hold on the Power button and seiect Power Lines again.

Place power lines across the roads to connect all parts of each zone.

Now sit patiently for a few minutes as your city slowly begins to grow.

Note: If nobody moves into your city, then it's either because the zones aren't powered up, or the residential and industrial zones are too far apart. Sims like to drive their cars, but they hate to commute very far.

Your Just Desserts

Your city should be growing now. Go ahead and add some more zones, or play with roads to get in some practice. Fairly soon a newspaper will announce to the world that your little town has reached the lofty population of 2000, and as a reward, you may build yourself a house.

Note: If you don't get this message after 5 or 7 minutes, then you may not have made your zones large enough.

This is but the first of many rewards that you will reap as mayor of SimCity. Rewards are based on population, and include your own house, a city hall, a statue in your honor and ... well, you'll find out.

Rewards show up under the Reward button in the City toolbar, which is ghosted and unavailable most of the time. Once you reach the population of 2000, then the Reward button will no longer be ghosted.

Click and hold on the Reward button, slide the cursor to Mayor's House and release the mouse button.

Place your house in a prestigious spot, preferably with a good view.

Connect your house to the rest of the town with roads and power lines.

Congratulations. You've successfully taken a hunk of barren dirt and built a small city. But this is no time to rest on your laurels. For now, save your city to disk, then we'll move on.

Open the File menu.

Select Save City.

Depending on your computer, it will either go ahead and save without asking you any questions, or prompt you for a location and file name. See your machine-specific Addendum for details on saving files and file names.

An aware planner is a steward of the earth, whose designs enhance the natural evolution of a place instead of inhibiting it. If you move to a mountain, then live on the mountain—don't try to turn it into a valley. If you move to the desert, live in and with the desert—don't pretend it's something else and plant yards with water-hungry grass.

VI

SIM CITY 2000

Belly on Up to the [Tool]Bar

Let's take a quick look at the City toolbar. If it ever gets in your way you can move it around the screen by clicking and dragging the bar at the top.

An important—and useful—thing to remember is the built-in help. Just hold down either Shift key, and click on any button in the toolbar for a complete explanation of what the button does.

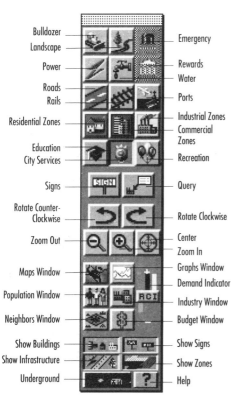

Bulldozer
Landscape
Power
Roads
Rails
Residential Zones
Education
City Services
Signs
Rotate Counter-Clockwise
Zoom Out
Maps Window
Population Window
Neighbors Window
Show Buildings
Show Infrastructure
Underground

Emergency
Rewards
Water
Ports
Industrial Zones
Commercial Zones
Recreation
Query
Rotate Clockwise
Center
Zoom In
Graphs Window
Demand Indicator
Industry Window
Budget Window
Show Signs
Show Zones
Help

All of the buttons in the top five rows activate submenus that give the button more power and flexibility. You've already seen that with the Power button.

Click and hold on all the buttons in the top five rows, one by one, to see all their submenus.

Two of the buttons will not do anything: the Reward button and the Emergency button. The Emergency button, which lets you dispatch police and fire departments to the scene of an emergency, only works during an emergency. And as you already know, the Reward button only lights up as you reach certain population levels.

Seeing all those submenus should assure you that there's a lot more to mastering SimCity 2000 than building a town of 2000 people. Many of these features will be covered in Tutorial 3, but there are a few items that will prove useful to you right away: the bulldozer, landscaping and building bridges.

The bulldozer has a number of uses, but for now we'll concentrate on its Demolish/Clear function.

Click and hold on the Bulldozer button.

Highlight Demolish/Clear.

Now go on a rampage through your city. Bulldoze any extra sections of road, abandoned factories or anything else you'd care to eliminate. (Don't worry, the city has been saved to disk, you can undo any damage you do by loading it back in.)

The first time you 'doze something, it turns it to rubble (with quite a jolly explosion). 'Doze it again to clear the rubble.

The Landscape button lets you add trees or water to the landscape. Click and hold on the Landscape button.

Highlight Trees and release the mouse button.

Click or click and drag across the land to add trees.

Trees add value to land as well as an aesthetic touch to your creation. Now for water.

Click and hold on the Landscape button.

Highlight Water and release the mouse button.

Click or click and drag across the land to make a small lake—but keep it small, adding water is expensive.

Water also adds value to land, and has recreational value, too.

Doin' Some Dozin'

Over the River and Through the Woods

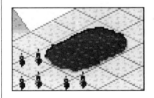

A Little Bridgework

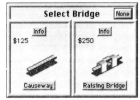

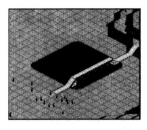

And speaking of water, how do you make your roads cross it?

Locate and center the screen on a lake or river that has flat land surrounding it.

Click on the Road button.

Click and drag the cursor so it crosses the lake or river.

Just by laying a road over water, the SimConstruction crew knows that you need a bridge. So they pop up this dialog box to let you decide what kind of bridge you want and tell you how much it'll cost. There is also an Info button you can press for more information on each type of bridge. Depending on the year in your city, and the width of the water, you will be shown a choice of one, two or three different bridges you can build. For now, go ahead and build a causeway bridge.

Click on the Causeway button to build the bridge.

The causeway is only one of the three types of bridges that you can have in SimCity 2000. Let's build another one, or two if they are all available.

Click and drag across the water next to the causeway.

When given the choice of bridges, build a raising bridge, if it is available.

Now build a suspension bridge if it is available.

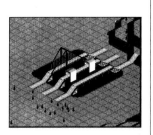

Ancient civilizations often identified their places with a particular deity that personified its distinctive qualities.

VIII

A handy-dandy feature of SimCity 2000 is the ability to add signs to buildings or spots of interest in your city.

Click on the Sign button.

Click on one of the bridges you just built.

Type "Orthodontist's Dream" into the dialog box.

Click the Done button.

Give Me a Sign

At the bottom of the City toolbar are six buttons. The one with the question mark brings up a reminder that you can get help on each button of the toolbar by holding down the Shift key and clicking on the button.

Show and Tell

To the left of the help button is the Underground button. Clicking on it reveals SimCity's soft white underbelly, where you can build an underground transportation system and run water to all your city's buildings. Clicking on it again takes you back up to the surface.

The four buttons above Help and Underground are Show Buildings, Show Signs, Show Infrastructure and Show Zones. Each of these buttons toggles on and off different parts of the city. The parts aren't destroyed, they just turn invisible until you want to see them again.

Zoom out, center on the built-up part of your city and play with the four Show buttons, the Underground button and the Help button for a while.

Hang in there. We're almost done with Tutorial 1!

The sizes of most early cities around the world were originally determined by the capacity of surrounding farmlands to feed the population. Many modern urban planners are aware of the importance of determining how large a population can be sustained within the boundaries of a municipality. But then again, many aren't.

IX

You're in Demand

Now take a look at the City toolbar and pick out the Demand Indicator. This lets you know what type of zones are in demand in your city. The bars stick up to show demand and down to show oversupply for Residential, Commercial and Industrial zones.

What a Pane

To the left of the Demand Indicator are six buttons. Each of these buttons opens small information windows that sit on top of the City window. The information in these windows helps you understand what's going on in your city, and helps you keep things running smoothly. Some of them will be covered in Tutorial 3. All of them are explained in detail in the Reference section.

Most of these buttons (all but the one with the money sign) work in two ways:

Maps Window

Graphs Window

Industry Window

Budget Window

Neighbors Window

Population Window

1. Click and hold on them to see a small pop-up information display that disappears when you let go of the mouse button.

2. Click and drag them away from the toolbar to open a window that stays until you tell it to go away.

One at a time, click and hold on each of the six buttons, take a quick look at what comes up, then release the mouse button. (Note that the Budget window stays there unless you click the Done button.)

One at a time, click and drag each of the six buttons to open all the windows.

Close all the windows.

Well, that's it for Tutorial 1. When you're ready for more, check out the next two tutorials. And the Reference section is always there when you need it for details on every window, toolbar and button. Now go play.

Play.

Have fun.

Have more fun.

Welcome back. In this tutorial, we'll be modifying and customizing the landforms that you build your cities on.

Tutorial 2— Landscape Engineering

In the last tutorial we touched on adding trees and water with the Landscape button, and looked at the submenu under the Bulldozer button. These are powerful tools for molding, shaping and beautifying the land. But if you make drastic changes, it can drain your city's treasury.

All the time you spent in Tutorial 1 was in "City-Building mode." As an alternative, SimCity 2000 has a "Terrain-Editing mode" that allows you to make all the modifications to the land you want—at no charge—before you actually start your city. When you've created the perfect locale for a new town, you can switch to City mode and start building. But you can't switch back. Sorry, them's the rules.

Enough gabbing. Put on your work boots and grab your hard hat—we've got mountains to move.

The attitude of the ancient Greeks toward town design reflects their sense of the finite, the idea that all things should be a definite size to be comprehensible and workable. Aristotle described the ideal size of a city, or "polis," noting that less than 10,000 people are too few to constitute a viable political entity and more than 20,000 are too unwieldy.

X

In the Mode

First, we'll get into Terrain-Editing mode.

If SimCity 2000 isn't running now, start it up. You'll soon see this dialog box:

Load Saved City
Start New City
Edit New Map
Load Scenario

Click Edit New Map.

If SimCity 2000 is already running, and you've been playing for a while, save whatever you're working on (if you wish) and:

Click on the Zoom Out button until you are all the way out.

Open the File menu.

Select Edit New Map.

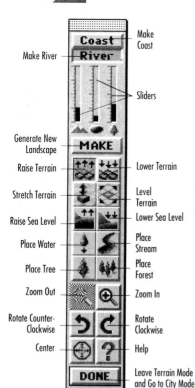

Make Coast

Make River

Sliders

Generate New Landscape

Raise Terrain — Lower Terrain

Stretch Terrain — Level Terrain

Raise Sea Level — Lower Sea Level

Place Water — Place Stream

Place Tree — Place Forest

Zoom Out — Zoom In

Rotate Counter-Clockwise — Rotate Clockwise

Center — Help

Leave Terrain Mode and Go to City Mode

This is the same old City window as in Tutorial 1, but with a big difference—this time we're in Terrain mode, and the City toolbar has been replaced by the Terrain toolbar.

Near the bottom of the toolbar are six buttons that you are already familiar with. The Zoom In, Zoom Out, Rotate, Center and Help buttons work here exactly as they do in the City toolbar.

And, of course, if you ever need a reminder of what a button does, hold down either Shift key and click on the button.

The top section of the Terrain toolbar gives you a good head start on reaching that perfect landform by letting you select some general characteristics that you want, then generating the land to your specifications. Once generated, you can customize it to your heart's content.

The Coast button lets you choose to (or not to) have an ocean coastline along one side of your city.

The River button lets you choose whether or not a river runs through it.

The three slider bars let you set how much of the land you want to be covered by mountains, water and trees. To set the slider bars, you can either click and drag them or just click at your desired setting. The higher the bar, the more mountain, water and tree coverage.

When you've finished with the Coast and River buttons and the sliders, clicking on the Make button generates the new landform.

To test it out, try generating landforms with each of these settings:

Set the buttons and sliders to match example one, to the right.

Click on the Make button.

Look over the landscape.

Repeat for the other two examples.

1   2

With the two buttons and three sliders you can create an almost unlimited number of landforms. Play around with generating landforms for a while if you wish, then generate the landform from example 3.

3

SIM CITY 2000

Did the Earth Move for You, too?

You should be looking at something approximately like this:

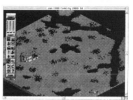

Note: As you go through the rest of this tutorial, feel free to zoom in for a closer look and rotate to get a different angle on your creation. You already know how to do it, so I won't bore you with the details.

Look over the terrain and pick a nice, big, flat, boring spot. We'll use the Raise Terrain tool to give it a lift.

Click on the Raise Terrain button.

Click and drag on a flat spot of land to build a huge mountain.

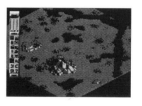

Making Molehills out of Mountains

Well, maybe that mountain is a bit too high for this flat, prairie-like wilderness. Let's bring it down with the Lower Terrain tool.

Click on the Lower Terrain button.

Trim the mountain down to size

    —but not too small.

Sometimes you need to flatten out the top of a mountain and form terraces to make some usable, level space. That's where the Level Terrain tool comes in.

Note: If you don't have enough of your mountain left after lowering it, use the Raise Terrain tool to build it back up again.

Click on the Level Terrain button.

Click and hold somewhere on your mountain near—but not at—the top.

Drag the cursor across the top of the mountain to chop it off.

  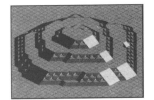

You probably noticed that the Level Terrain tool raises land to your chosen level as well as lowers it. Now make some terraces on your mountain.

When you do a lot of terrain modifications, you will sometimes see grey triangular areas. These are actually cement supports to keep the land from shifting or caving in. SimConstruction engineers are trained professionals who know how to do their jobs.

Even in today's world, we seek relationships to neighborhoods of less than 20,000 people, beyond which we lose our ability to relate to the rest of the population. We need to be able to identify with those who live near us, or else we feel "lost."

XI

A Bit of a Stretch

The Stretch Terrain tool lets you grab a section of land and stretch it up into a mountain or pull it down to a mesa or canyon.

Locate a flat, empty section of land.

Click on the Stretch Terrain tool.

Click and hold on the land, drag it upwards to create a pyramid-like mountain, and release the mouse button.

Click on the top of the mountain and drag it down to flatten it into a mesa.

Click and hold on the side of the mountain and drag the cursor down to carve out a canyon.

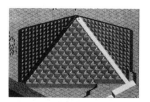

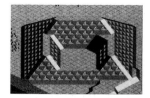

Large metropolises tend to separate and concentrate elements of business necessities and cultural amenities, eliminating diversity within neighborhoods. Smaller cities retain a greater potential for mixed experiences, which invigorates nature's most adaptable creature: man.

XII

Water You Thinkin' About?

Enough of this dealing with dirt—let's get wet. There are a few water tools in the Terrain toolbar. One works just like the Water setting on the Landscape button in the City toolbar. The other is a little more powerful—and little more unpredictable. It lets you place flowing streams.

Find or build a small hill somewhere in the terrain.

Click on the Water button.

Click and drag on the flat terrain at the foot of the hill.

Click on the Place Stream button.

Click at the top of the hill to send a stream running down into the lake.

Click a few more times in the same area to produce a cascading waterfall.

There are also buttons that let you raise and lower sea level.

Click on the Zoom Out button until you are all the way out.

Click once on the Raise Sea Level button.

Click twice on the Lower Sea Level button.

Click again on the Raise Sea Level button.

These buttons let you turn mountains into a chain of islands, turn wet grassland into a desert, or create swampland if you know any rich suckers.

Out In the Woods

SimCity 2000 lets you add trees and forests to your landscape, with (of all things) the Tree and Forest buttons.

Find a spot in the terrain that is sadly lacking trees.

Click on the Tree button.

Click and drag across the barren plain to plant some trees.

Click on the Forest button.

Click and drag across the plain to plant a lot of trees.

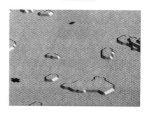

City a la Mode

You are now the master of land, sea and forest, able to shape them to suit your whims. If you wish, take some time and play around with the landscape. When you're ready to get a city going, then head for the Done button at the bottom of the Terrain toolbar. It sends you into City mode, changes the toolbar, and starts time in the city.

Click Done and start building a city.

You'll find the Raise Terrain, Lower Terrain and Level Terrain functions in the submenu under the Bulldozer button. But remember: in City mode, you'll be charged for each tile you raise, lower or level.

If and when you feel like it, Tutorial 3 is just around the corner, filled with useful advanced city-building techniques.

Tutorial 3— Advanced Features

If you're here then you must already be an experienced mayor with complete mastery of all the tools and techniques in Tutorials 1 and 2. Either that or you're so excited about the advanced features of SimCity 2000 that you just couldn't wait.

In any event, in this tutorial, you will:

- Load in your old city from Tutorial 1.
- Take a look around with the Query tool.
- Add police and fire protection.
- Take a quick look at all the smaller windows and get an idea of what they do.
- Play with the Budget window and city finance.
- Make a couple political deals in the Council window.
- Deal with an emergency.

A New Beginning

If SimCity 2000 isn't running now, start it up. You'll soon see this dialog box:

Click Load Saved City.

Load your city from the end of Tutorial 1.

If SimCity 2000 is already running, and you've been playing for a while, save whatever you're working on (if you wish) and:

Open the File menu.

Select Load City.

Load your city from the end of Tutorial 1.

> *Note: Loading cities is a little different for each type of computer. See your machine-specific Addendum for details.*

SIM CITY 2000

Within seconds, you will be looking over the familiar landscape of Tutorial 1 City. Before moving on, let's do a couple things: turn on Auto-Budget to keep that pesky Budget window away until we're ready for it, and add some police and fire protection to your town.

Open the Options menu.

Select Auto-Budget (unless it's already on).

Click and hold on the City Services button in the City toolbar.

Select Police from the submenu.

Place the police station somewhere in your city.

Click and hold on the City Services button again.

Select Fire Station from the submenu.

Place a fire station somewhere in your city, possibly near the police station.

Make sure the stations have power and access to roads.

The Query Theory

Inquiring mayors want and need to know what's going on in their towns. And whether you need to research important city issues or are just curious, the Query tool gives you the low-down on your city.

Click on the Query button in the City toolbar.

Click on a house in your residential zone.

An information box has popped up with all the vital stats the simulator has about the spot where you clicked.

Click on the information box to close it.

Click on your police station.

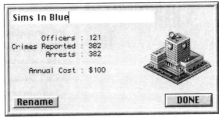

Once again an information box has opened, but this time with different information—information that is important in judging the effectiveness of a police station. Whenever you query a place in your city, you will see the most useful information for that place. Pay attention to the numbers of officers, crimes and arrests in this box, and scribble them down on a piece of paper if you have one handy. Later on we'll see what cutting the police budget does to these numbers.

Notice the Rename button. SimCity 2000 allows you to personalize your city by renaming many of the buildings and locations.

Click on the Rename button.

Type in your own name for your police department, something like, "Tutorial Enforcement Unit," or "Sims In Blue."

Click the Done button.

When business, culture and leisure overlap, creative energies flow though our streets, our shops, our homes. Under diversified conditions, society becomes richer in experiences and civilizations continue to unfold.

XIII

A WhirlWind[ow] Tour

Other than a brief glimpse at the other windows in Tutorial 1, we've spent almost the whole time in the City window. The City window is the mainstay of SimCity 2000. It stays active even when other windows are open on top of it. Clicking on the City window won't bring it to the front, covering any of the other, smaller windows on the screen. When you place the other windows, try not to cover the City window's Scroll bars.

After the City window, the Map window is the most-used and most versatile.

Click and drag the Map window button in the City toolbar away from the toolbar to open the Map window.

Click in the Grow box in the upper right corner to enlarge the Map window.

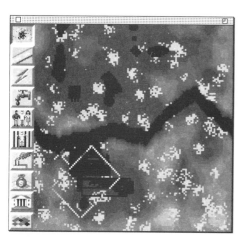

Welcome to the Map window. It shows a number of different map displays that give you location-based information about your city. You can open it either through the Windows menu or with the Map window button in the City toolbar.

Somewhere on the map is a white rectangle. The rectangle shows the area of the map that is currently visible in the City window. When you click on the map, you move the rectangle, and the City window redraws to show the new area in the rectangle.

Click on the map a few times to move the rectangle, and see how the City window changes.

Click on the map, over the middle of your city.

The buttons along the left side of the Map window let you choose different map displays. Some of the buttons have submenus for even more displays. Let's take a quick look at all the map displays.

Note: In map displays that show density or coverage, the darker the greyscale, the higher the density.

Click and hold on the top Map window button.

Select the first item in the submenu and release the mouse button. Take a look at the map.

Repeat for every item of every submenu of every Map window button—except the very last button. (Don't worry, it won't take very long; some of the buttons don't have submenus.)

The last Map window button doesn't change the view in the Map window—it turns the City window into a super-duper-extra-large map. (This is the City window's Map mode.) Clicking the button again returns the City window to its normal state. Sometimes you need a huge, detailed map to see all the finer details of your city.

Click on the last Map window button.

Take a look, then click on it again.

Click in the Close box to close the Map window.

The Graphs window shows time-based information about the people, places and problems in your city. Use it for identifying and tracking trends and changes in things like pollution, land value, and levels of health and education. You can open it from the Windows menu or by clicking and dragging the Graphs window button in the City toolbar.

Click and drag the Graphs window button on the City toolbar to open the Graphs window.

Spend 2 minutes and 37 seconds turning on and off each of the graphs, and changing the scale from 1 to 10 to 100 years.

Close the Graphs window.

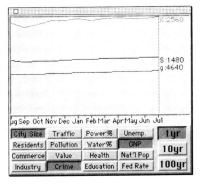

The Population window gives you information about the people in your city, and their levels of health and education. You can open the Population window in the usual ways.

Click and drag the Population window button on the City toolbar.

Click on each of the three buttons at the bottom of the window and look at each of the three displays.

Close the Population window.

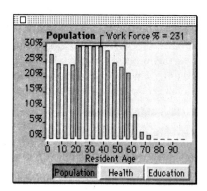

The Industries window shows the ratio of the different types of industries in your city. It also shows which industries' products are in demand nationally, and allows you to set different tax rates for each industry to encourage, discourage or drain dry those industries you like, don't like or just want to exploit. You can open the Industries window by... you know the routine by now.

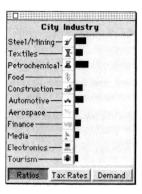

Click and drag the Industries window button in the City toolbar.

Look over the current (Population) display.

Click on the Tax Rates button.

Pick an industry you want to encourage, and lower its tax rate by clicking and dragging its bar toward the left.

Pick an industry you want to discourage, and raise its tax rate by clicking and dragging its bar toward the right.

Click on the Demand button and look over the Demand display.

Close the Industries window.

The Neighbors window shows your city surrounded by its neighboring cities, and gives the populations for each city, and for SimNation as a whole. I bet you can figure out how the Neighbors window is opened.

Open the Windows menu and select Neighbors (unless you really really want to use the Neighbors window button).

Take a look and close the window.

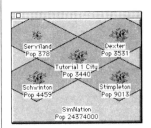

The Budget window is where you control all the finances of your city. The Budget window is so important that it deserves its own clever headline in this tutorial, so here goes:

Click on the Budget window button in the City toolbar.

Along the left side of the Budget window is a list of all the revenues and expenses that you face as a mayor in SimCity 2000. For each revenue or expense, there is:

The Buck Starts Here

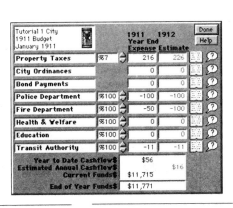

- Year-to-Date Column—a number (in blue) that shows the actual cash amount you have made or spent so far this year.

- Estimated Column—a number (in red) that shows what the end-of-year expense or revenue will be at the current Budget window settings.

- Books—a button to push to see a detailed monthly report on the revenue or expense.

- Advisors—a button to push when you want a little advice.

- Percentages—most (but not all) of the revenues and expenses have a percentage setting so you can set the amounts of funding or taxation.

Help is available by holding down either Shift key and clicking on any word, number, column or button in the Budget window.

The very first revenue is your main source of income: property taxes. To the right of the words "Property Taxes" is the current tax rate given as a percentage (currently 7%). You can set the property tax rate to anything between 0 and 20% by clicking on the up and down arrows to the right of the percentage number. Give your Sims a break and lower their taxes.

Click twice on the down-arrow to the right of Property Taxes and lower the rate to 5%.

If your computer is equipped to play sound effects, you'll hear the cheers of the populace.

Click once on the up-arrow to the right of Property Taxes and raise the rate to 6%.

Once again, if your computer can play sound effects, you'll hear the reaction of the masses. How soon they forget.

Skip down to Bond Payment. This is the amount of interest you pay on bond issues. Part of financing your city is issuing bonds, which is basically borrowing money from your citizens. The interest rate the city pays varies according to the simulated market and the difficulty level of the game. Everything you need to deal with bonds is in the Bond Payment books.

As technology and waves of immigration advanced, laws became necessary to minimize fire damage in congested areas and to assure a supply of drinking water as well as to carry away sewage. With our ability to build higher, faster and "better," we also realized that neighbors could affect each other's property values and aesthetics.

XIV

Click on the Book button for Bond Payment.

The Bond Payment books give you a month-by-month breakdown of the number of outstanding bonds, their interest rate, the monetary amount of interest you pay and a total of interest paid. Blue numbers show actual year-to-date amounts, red numbers are projections for the rest of the year.

Month	Bond$	Rate%	Cost$	Total$
Jan	$0	0.0%	$0	$0
Feb	$0	0.0%	$0	$0
Mar	$0	0.0%	$0	$0
Apr	$0	0.0%	$0	$0
May	$0	0.0%	$0	$0
Jun	$0	0.0%	$0	$0
Jul	$0	0.0%	$0	$0
Aug	$0	0.0%	$0	$0
Sep	$0	0.0%	$0	$0
Oct	$0	0.0%	$0	$0
Nov	$0	0.0%	$0	$0
Dec	$0	0.0%	$0	$0

| Show Bonds | Issue Bond | Repay Bond | Done |

At the bottom of the window are buttons for dealing with bond issues.

Click on the Show Bonds button.

You are shown a pop-up box with your city's credit rating, and general status on bonds and interest rates.

```
Loan Rating:    AAA        Outstanding Bonds
Total Bonds:    0
Bank Rate%:     11%
Next Bond%:     12%

City Value: $4,000,000
```

Click on the pop-up box to close it.

Click on the Issue Bond button.

You are given the current bond interest rate and asked if you want to issue the bond. Go ahead.

```
Current Rates are 12%
Do You Want to Issue the Bond?
  Yes          No
```

Click Yes to issue the bond.

Click on the Show Bonds button to see that it has been issued.

Click to close the Show Bonds box.

Later, when you have the money, you can come back here and repay the bond, but for now, let's move on.

Click the Done button to close the Bond Payment books and return to the Budget window.

Look at the line just below Bond Payment. This is the financial information for your Police Departments. To the right of the words "Police Department" is a percentage number set to 100, and to the right of that are up-and down-arrows that let you change the level of funding.

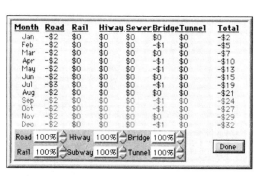

Click on the down-arrow to change the Police Department funding to 50%.

Click on the Police Department Book button.

Look it over, then click to close the Police books.

We'll check out the effect of lowering the police budget a little later. There are no other buttons or adjustments in the Police books.

Let's look at another set of books.

Click on the Transit Authority Book button.

Month	Police	Fund	Cost	Total
Jan	1	100%	-$8	-$8
Feb	1	100%	-$8	-$16
Mar	1	100%	-$9	-$25
Apr	1	100%	-$8	-$33
May	1	50%	-$4	-$37
Jun	1	50%	-$4	-$41
Jul	1	50%	-$4	-$45
Aug	1	50%	-$5	-$50
Sep	1	50%	-$4	-$54
Oct	1	50%	-$4	-$58
Nov	1	50%	-$4	-$62
Dec	1	50%	-$4	-$66

Not only do the Transit Authority books give you a monthly breakdown of transit expenses, but they let you individually set the funding levels for different transportation systems. Since the bridges we built in Tutorial 1 aren't hooked up to anything, there's no point in funding them. And just to see what happens, we'll remove funding from a couple other systems.

Click on the down-arrow for Bridge funding until it goes to 0%.

Set funding levels for Subway and Tunnel to 0%.

Click Done to close the Transit Authority books and return to the Budget window.

Notice that the percentage setting next to Transit Authority changed. When you change settings in the books, they are reflected here.

One more set of books to inspect: City Ordinance (just under Property Taxes).

Page 42   *SimCity 2000 — Tutorial*

Click on the City Ordinance Book button.

These are various programs, bills and ordinances that you can enact as mayor. Each program contributes in some way to the quality of life in your city, but each also has a drawback, usually its cost. Politics is a rough business, filled with hard decisions.

That's it for the Budget window—except for one detail. Let's clear out all this budget stuff then see how our funding change affected the police department.

Click Done to close the Community Program dialog.

Click Done to close the Budget window.

Click on the Query button in the City toolbar.

Click on the Police Department.

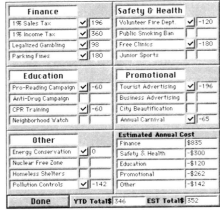

When you compare it with your last query, you should have about half as many officers. Depending on the size of your city, crime may be running rampant, or it may be under control. In a very small town, you don't necessarily need full police or fire department funding.

And speaking of fire departments...

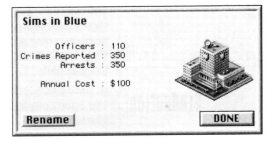

From time to time, or when you feel like it, you will have the solemn duty (or distinct pleasure, depending on your personality) of dealing with disasters. Of course, the best way to deal with a disaster is to prevent it. The better fire coverage you have, the less often fires will occur. But sometimes, no matter how prepared you are, disaster strikes. Especially when you choose them from a menu.

A Hot Time in the Old Town

Open the Disasters menu.

Select Fire.

Once you select Fire, two things will happen: a fire will break out somewhere in the city limits and the Emergency button will become available. The Emergency tool lets you dispatch your police and fire departments to the scene of the emergency.

Click and hold on the Emergency button in the City toolbar.

Select Dispatch Fire.

Click near the fire.

Click and hold on the Emergency button.

Select Dispatch Police.

Click near the fire.

> *Note: If the fire went out before you had a chance to dispatch your troops, start another one.*

You can't place your fire fighters directly on fires, but you can use them to block the path of the fire, and even chase it down. You can place one police or fire icon for every station you have. If you have three of four stations, it makes it easier to surround a fire and block its path.

Graduation

You have completed an extensive tutorial in city design and management. You are now an expert in everything from planning to landscaping to politics.

When you're ready for even more advanced features, check out the Reference section for tips on adding a water system to your city, and improving and expanding your transportation system with highways, onramps, tunnels, rails, subways, and bus lines.

Go forth and play SimCity 2000.

REFERENCE

Slums may well be breeding-grounds of crime, but middle-class suburbs are incubators of apathy and delirium.
The Unquiet Grave

– Cyril Connolly (1903-1974)

Reference

This Reference section is an in-depth explanation of (just about) every window, button, feature and function of SimCity 2000 on a number of different computers. This section will make a lot more sense to you if you play through Tutorial 1 first.

The Basics

Here are a few basic points that should clarify your place in the SimCity 2000 universe and prepare you for the rest of the Reference section.

Who Are You and What Are You Doing?

In SimCity 2000 you are the planner and mayor of an unlimited number of cities. These cities can be as small as you want or as large as you can make them.

Your cities don't live in a vacuum. Their growth and decline are affected by surrounding cities. These surrounding cities are both a market for selling your manufactured goods and competitors, vying for population and businesses.

In your role as mayor, you are directly responsible for:
- Planning—zoning, long- and short-range strategies
- City infrastructure—water, power, transportation
- Government services—fire, police, hospitals, prisons
- Education—schools, colleges, libraries, museums
- Recreation and open spaces—parks, zoos, stadiums, marinas
- City budget and taxes
- Major and minor land manipulation
- The health, wealth and happiness of the Sims that live in your city

You are not directly responsible for building houses, stores, factories or other buildings (the Sims take care of them).

Scenarios and Cities

There are a number of scenarios built into SimCity 2000. Each scenario provides you with different challenges at different levels of difficulty.

Each scenario has a "win" condition. If you meet this condition within a specific time, you'll receive the key to the city and be allowed to continue your job as mayor. If you don't meet the condition, you'll be run out of town—until you're ready to try again.

When you start your own city, there are no time limits to beat and no conditions to meet. There is no winning or losing. You are the sole judge, passing judgment upon yourself. The only two criteria in this judgment are your own enjoyment and the quality of life of your Sims.

SimCity 2000 on Different Computers

Each computer platform has its own rules and conventions for terminology, menu use, keyboard use, mouse use, file loading and saving, and windowing. We have kept SimCity 2000 as consistent from computer to computer as we could while staying true to each computer's interface. In those few places where things differ greatly from computer to computer, you will be referred to the machine-specific Addendum.

The graphics for this manual were taken from the Macintosh version of SimCity 2000. If there are any differences between the graphics in the manual and the graphics on your screen, see the machine-specific Addendum.

In 1916, New York City adopted a zoning ordinance which would become the model for cities across the nation. Overcrowding, overdevelopment, adverse effects on neighboring property values, lack of light and air became matters of public health... and a new public agency was created to safeguard the public by regulating and controlling development. "Public health, welfare and safety" became the accepted basis for regulation by municipalities.

XV

SIM CITY 2000

Mouse and Keyboard Conventions

In general, all instructions that refer to clicking, double-clicking or clicking and dragging refer to the left mouse button (if you have more than one).

Things that are done on the Mac by holding down the Option key while clicking, are done on DOS- and Windows-based computers by holding down the Control key and clicking.

Getting Help

Help is available in most places in SimCity 2000. If you see a button with a question mark on it, click on it for help.

If you have a mouse with more than one button, clicking with the right button on any button or icon will invoke a help message explaining that button or icon. If you have a mouse with one button, hold down either Shift key on your keyboard and click on any button or icon for help.

Terrain

Terrain in SimCity 2000 has 32 levels of altitude, with mountains, valleys, lakes, rivers, streams, and waterfalls. You can customize and modify the landform, both at the beginning of a game and during actual city-building.

When you start a brand-new city with the Edit New Map command from the File menu, you can mold and shape the terrain for your city as much as you want, without any charge. Once you start playing a game and begin building a city, it will cost you to modify the terrain.

The land is divided up into "tiles." A tile is the smallest piece of land that can be raised, lowered or covered with water. It is approximately 200 by 200 feet square, or about one acre.

City Limits

The total city limits are equivalent to approximately 5 miles by 5 miles square. Buildings, objects, roads, etc., are also divided up into tiles. One section of road is one tile. Some of the larger buildings are made of many tiles.

The entire city limits is yours for city expansion, for parks and open spaces, or to leave wild. A city in SimCity 2000 can be tiny, or can fill the entire rectangular city limits.

You can build multiple separate communities or small cities within the city limits, but the simulation will treat them as one city. All the statistics and information in the Graphs, Population, Industry and other windows collectively covers everything within the entire city limits.

The City Window and the Rest of 'Em

The City window is your main view of your city. It is always open as long as SimCity 2000 is running. The game is easiest to control with the City window as large as possible, but you can resize it on some computers.

Most of the other, smaller windows, such as the Map and Population windows, open either by selecting them in the Windows menu, or by clicking on their button on the toolbar.

If you just want to take a quick look at one of the smaller windows (momentary view), click and hold on their buttons in the toolbar. The window will be visible until you release the mouse button. If, while holding down the button, you drag the window away from the toolbar then release the mouse button, then the window will remain on the screen until you close it (tear-off view).

There are two other important points to remember about the small windows:

1. Some of them have extra buttons or controls that appear in tear-off, but not momentary view.

2. As long as these small windows are open, they will remain on top of the City window. When you click on the City window to modify the city, it will not cover the small windows—place them carefully so they don't block your access to the City window scroll bars.

Menus

These are all the menus and menu items in SimCity 2000. There may be a few slight differences on different computers.

File Menu

This menu has the commands for file management, starting new games and scenarios and quitting SimCity 2000.

ABOUT SIMCITY 2000
Brings up exciting and thrilling information about the game and its makers. If your computer has a special menu, like the Macintosh "Apple" menu, this item will be there and not in the File menu.

LOAD CITY
Opens a file-loading dialog box allowing you to load in and play a previously saved SimCity 2000 city. This command can also be used to import a city from SimCity or SimCity Classic.

NEW CITY
First asks if you want to save your existing city, then generates a new, empty terrain, prompts you for the city's name and game level, then begins the game.

EDIT NEW MAP
First asks you if you want to save your existing city, then removes all buildings and infrastructure and delivers the bare terrain into Terrain-Editing mode. In Terrain-Editing mode, you have access to tools to customize and/or regenerate the terrain to your heart's content—without being charged.

LOAD SCENARIO
Opens a dialog box that allows you to view all the different scenarios, then select one.

SAVE CITY
Saves the current city to disk under the same name and in the same place where it was last saved. If it hasn't been saved before, the Save City As... dialog box will open, allowing you to name/rename the city and choose the destination disk and directory or folder.

SAVE CITY AS...
Opens a dialog box that allows you to name/rename a city and choose the disk and directory or folder where you want to save it.

QUIT
Rips SimCity from your computer's memory and makes it go away until you're ready to resume your mayoral responsibilities. It will first ask if you want to save your existing city.

SPEED MENU
This menu has the commands for setting the simulation to different speeds, including pause. The currently set speed will be marked by a check mark. Actual speeds will vary, depending on your computer, its microprocessor and its clock speed.

PAUSE
Stops time in the simulation.

TURTLE
Sets the simulation to run slower than molasses on a cold day.

LLAMA
Sets the simulation to run at a medium speed.

CHEETAH
Sets the simulation to run as fast as your computer will go.

Options Menu

This menu controls a number of simulation and sound options so you can tailor the game to your style of play. Options that are active have a check mark next to them.

AUTO-BUDGET
When selected, Auto-Budget stops the Budget window from opening at the end of each year, and automatically repeats the previous budget.

AUTO-GOTO

When active, Auto-Goto automatically centers the City window over an important occurrence, such as a disaster. When inactive, you will still receive messages to notify you of important goings-on in your city.

SOUND EFFECTS

Toggles sound effects on and off. The audio quality of the sound effects will vary greatly depending on the sound capabilities of your computer.

MUSIC

Toggles the musical soundtrack on and off. The audio quality of the music will vary greatly depending on the sound capabilities of your computer.

Disasters Menu

This menu lets you activate various disasters, or disable them entirely. For more information on disasters, see Dealing with Disasters in the Strategies section below.

FIRE

Causes a fire to break out somewhere within the city limits.

FLOOD

Causes a wave of raised water to come in off the coast or down a river, washing away anything that isn't tied down.

AIR CRASH

Causes an airplane to crash somewhere within the city limits.

TORNADO

Sets a tornado loose to wreak havoc across the city limits.

EARTHQUAKE

Sets the earth to quakin' and the ground to shakin'.

MONSTER

Releases the terror of the year 2000.

NO DISASTERS

Prevents disasters from occurring. No Disasters will not prevent the "official" scenario disasters, or stop disasters already in progress. No Disasters also prevents the City Council from voting in ordinances without your approval.

Note: All power plants have a 50-year life span, and then they blow up. They don't cause fires or spread radiation—they just stop working and collapse. Watch your newspapers for warnings that power plants are getting old. If you have No Disasters active, when power plants reach the end of their lives, they are automatically rebuilt and you are automatically charged. If you don't have enough cash in your city funds to pay for the power plant replacement, it goes boom.

This menu lets you access the various windows in SimCity 2000.

Windows Menu

MAP

Opens the Map window for various displays of your entire city.

BUDGET

Opens the Budget window for fiddling with your city's finances.

ORDINANCES

Opens the Ordinance window for setting and inspecting various city bonds, bills and ordinances.

POPULATION

Opens the Population window to see a demographic breakdown of the Sims in your city.

INDUSTRY

Opens the Industry window to see the different types of industries currently operating in your city, and to set individual tax rates for different industries.

GRAPHS

Opens the Graphs window to see graphical displays of city data and statistics over time.

NEIGHBORS

Opens the Neighbors window to see how you compare with your surrounding neighbor cities.

Newspaper Menu

This menu lets you set your newspaper delivery rate and read various local papers. Even with both delivery options below turned off, newspapers announcing disasters will be delivered.

SUBSCRIPTION

When active, a newspaper will be delivered (popped up on the screen) twice a year.

EXTRA!!!

When active, only newspapers that report important occurrences—inventions and major steps in city growth—will be delivered.

THE NEWSPAPERS

Opens and/or activates the various local newspapers. There will be from none (at the start of a city) to six (in a very large city) different local newspapers. The newspaper that is marked with a circle to the left of its name is the paper that will be delivered. Opening a newspaper manually changes it to the one that will be delivered.

The creation of zoning and public health, welfare and safety laws was thought to be a solution to many problems: a benevolent public body enlightened to determine what is best for all and empowered through enabling legislation to enforce its findings. It would not take long, however, to realize that this new set of rules did not eliminate difficulties in development of land; it only gave the battlefield boundaries and suggested new implements of war. **XVI**

This section describes in detail each of the windows in SimCity 2000.

City Window

IN GENERAL

The City window is your main work area for molding, shaping and growing your city and the land under it. It is always open while SimCity 2000 is running (on most computers).

At the top of the window is the Title bar, containing the simulation date, the name of the city and your current funds. On the right end of the Titlebar is some sort of box or button (depending on your computer) for quickly resizing the window.

- On the Macintosh and on DOS-based computers, it is the Zoom box, which toggles the window between full-screen size and the last previously set window size.

- On a Windows-based computer, there will be two buttons. The Maximize button toggles the window between full-screen size and the last previously set window size. The Minimize button shrinks the window to an icon.

You can resize the City window by clicking and dragging the Resize box.

The Scroll Bars and Scroll Arrows let you move the city around in the City window.

The Toolbar provides all the tools you'll need to zone, build and run your city. It appears differently, depending on the mode you are in. And speaking of modes...

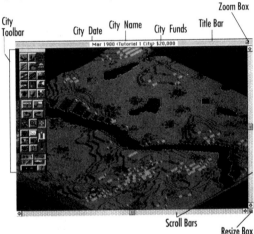

City Toolbar · City Date · City Name · City Funds · Title Bar · Zoom Box · Scroll Bars · Resize Box

MODES

The City window has three modes: City-Building, Terrain-Editing and Map.

City-Building is the main, most-used mode. It lets you build and grow your city. You can also edit the terrain, but there are physical and financial limitations.

In Terrain-Editing mode, you can make all the changes and modifications you could ever desire to the new, empty landscape without being charged. Once you leave Terrain-Editing mode and enter City-Building mode to start your city, you can never return that same landscape to Terrain-Editing mode.

Map mode turns the entire City window into a giant, scalable display that mirrors the information in the Map window. The City window's Map mode is toggled on and off from the Map window.

THE VIEW

The view in the City window is an isometric, simulated 3-D landscape. It can be viewed in three different sizes, allowing you to see more or less of your city at once, at various levels of detail.

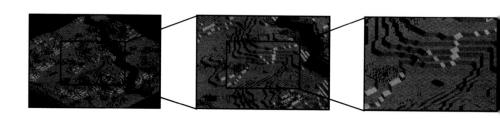

THE LANDSCAPE

Each time you start a new city in SimCity 2000, a new landscape is generated. You can regenerate the landscape as many times as you like. You can modify the landscape as much as you like.

When the City window is in terrain-editing mode, you can make drastic changes to the land at no cost to the city. You can raise or level mountains, dig streams, raise or lower the sea level, and place individual trees or forests.

Once the City window is in city-building mode, you can still make drastic changes to the landscape, but you'll have to pay for the work out of the city's funds.

There are three basic elements to the landscape: land, water and trees.

The land in SimCity 2000 is divided into small squares, called tiles. Tiles can be raised or lowered to provide 32 levels of altitude. Land that is below sea level will be under water.

Water in SimCity 2000 flows downhill, as all good water should. When you generate a new landscape in terrain-editing mode, you can choose whether or not you want a river running through the landscape, and you can, if you want, have one edge of your city be a coastline. Your landscape can also have streams, ponds and lakes. And you can raise or lower sea level, to make your city either a desert or a chain of islands.

Trees in SimCity 2000, as in the real world, are big plants that provide shade and homes for wildlife. They add an aesthetic touch to cities, and improve land value.

THE CITY TOOLBAR

When the City window is in city-building mode, it has the City toolbar—your main control center for building, modifying and running your city. It can be moved around your screen by clicking and dragging the bar at the top.

For ease of use, especially for newcomers to SimCity 2000, you can simply click on any button, then use the default setting of the tool. When you're ready for more power, more features and more flexibility, you can make use of the submenus that are hidden below many of the buttons. If you click and hold on a button with a submenu, the submenu will pop up, allowing you to access many more choices and options. The submenus, and their available options, change over the years, reflecting the available technology.

The City toolbar contains tools that let you:

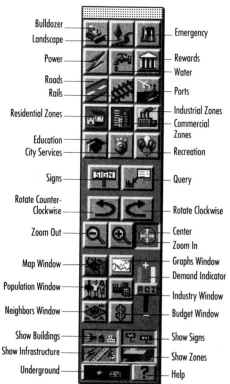

Bulldozer
Landscape
Power
Roads
Rails
Residential Zones
Education
City Services
Signs
Rotate Counter-Clockwise
Zoom Out
Map Window
Population Window
Neighbors Window
Show Buildings
Show Infrastructure
Underground

Emergency
Rewards
Water
Ports
Industrial Zones
Commercial Zones
Recreation
Query
Rotate Clockwise
Center
Zoom In
Graphs Window
Demand Indicator
Industry Window
Budget Window
Show Signs
Show Zones
Help

- Modify the landscape
- Zoom in and out for close-up and far-out views
- Center on different areas of the city in the City window
- Rotate the city in the City window
- Zone residential, commercial and industrial areas
- Build the city infrastructure
- Add special-purpose buildings (museums, zoos, etc.)
- Closely inspect city areas
- Add signs or markers
- Turn on and off the display of various objects and layers in the City window
- Open various information windows

It also has a Demand Indicator for various zones.

Any time you need a reminder of what each of the buttons does, hold down either Shift key and click on a button. A friendly help message will pop up and set you straight.

These are the tools in the City toolbar:

BULLDOZER

The bulldozer is a multi-function multi-level tool, with a default setting and a submenu to choose between four additional actions. Click and hold on the Bulldozer button to open the submenu. When the bulldozer is active, the cursor will appear as a bulldozer.

To operate the bulldozer, choose the function you want, then click or click and drag where you want to do your 'dozin'.

Demolish/Clear (the default) destroys and removes trees, rubble, and man-made (Sim-made?) objects without affecting the terrain or zoning status. Just click on anything to destroy it.
Cost: $1 per tile.

Level Terrain lets you choose an altitude level and slice off hills and mountains at your chosen height. Level also clears, removing all trees, roads, power lines and buildings.
Cost: $25 per tile per altitude change.

Raise Terrain lets you make mountains out of molehills.
Cost: $25 per tile per altitude change.

Lower Terrain lets you lower mountains and dig canyons. (If you lower the terrain below sea level, it will fill with water.)
Cost: $25 per tile per altitude change.

De-zone lets you change undeveloped residential, commercial or industrial zones to unzoned land.
Cost: $1 per tile.

Raising, lowering and leveling terrain can be very expensive, so do it sparingly. If you want to make a lot of changes to the landscape, do it in terrain-editing mode before you start your city, or save up a lot of cash.

LANDSCAPE TOOL

The Landscape tool lets you add trees and water to your city. When active, the cursor will appear as a tree. Clicking and holding on the button opens a submenu that allows you to choose between trees and water.

The Tree tool lets you place trees onto the landscape. Each click will place either one or two trees. You can click repeatedly on a single tile to create dense thickets, and click and drag across many tiles to create forests.

Cost: $3 per click.

The Water tool lets you create lakes and streams by clicking where you want your water to appear.

Cost: $100 per tile.

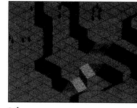
Before

After

EMERGENCY

The Emergency tool lets you dispatch police and/or fire departments to the scene of a disaster. This tool will be ghosted and unavailable unless a disaster is occurring. When active, the cursor will appear as an emergency beacon. Clicking and holding on the tool opens a submenu that allows you to choose between dispatching police and fire.

Once you activate the tool and choose the department you want to dispatch, click on the area of the city where you want your city's finest to go. An icon representing either your dispatched fire or police troops will be placed where you click. You can place one icon for each station you have. After you have placed them all,

clicking again will move the first one you placed to the last place you clicked, enabling you to block, surround and contain a fire or riot. There is no cost for dispatching police or firesims.

POWER

Power is a multi-use tool. Clicking and holding on it opens a submenu that allows you to choose between two functions: laying power lines and placing power plants. When this tool is active, the cursor appears as a lightning bolt.

Power Lines (the default setting) lets you "paint" your power lines onto the land by clicking in the place where you want the line to start, dragging the cursor to the place where you want the line to stop, and releasing the mouse button. If you start laying a power line and change your mind, you can cancel the operation by holding down the Shift key before you release the mouse button.

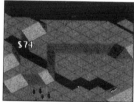

Click and drag...

Power lines blink warning lights to let you know if they're not hooked to a power source. Power lines can only be run in straight lines and 90-degree angles. They can cross roads or rails, but not on curved sections or straight sections that run at 45 degrees. Laying power lines across water is a little more expensive. If you lay power lines across water, a dialog box will open and let you know how much it will cost.

Cost: $2 per tile across land, $10 per tile across water.

and...release.

Power Plant... lets you choose power sources for your city. Depending on the year and the technology level of your city, there may be from three to nine types of power plants available. Click on the power source you want, then click on the terrain where you want it to go. There is an info button for each power plant that tells you the advantages, disadvantages and costs for each type of power plant.

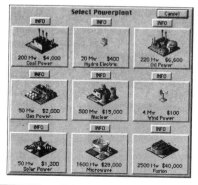

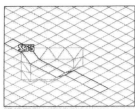

Click and drag...

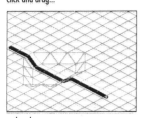

and...release.

WATER SYSTEM

The Water System tool is a multi-use tool. Clicking and holding on it opens a submenu that allows you to choose between five different water-related functions: laying water pipes, installing water pumps, buying storage tanks, and building treatment and desalinization plants. When this tool is active, the cursor appears as a water faucet.

Depending on the year and technology level in your city, you may only have access to pumps and water towers. As time passes and inventions are invented, the other options become available. A city can exist without a water system, but population density will be limited. When the Sims build, they install the underground water pipes for their buildings. Your only responsibility is to hook the buildings up to the water system.

Pipes (the default setting) lets you "paint" your water pipes onto the landscape by clicking in the place where you want the pipe to start, dragging the cursor to the place you want the pipe to stop, and releasing the mouse button. If you start laying a water pipe and change your mind, you can cancel the operation by holding down the Shift key before you release the mouse button. Water pipes are always laid underground. Activating Pipes automatically turns on the underground view so you can see your pipes. Cost: $3 per tile.

Water Pumps when placed on land act as wells, a good source of water. Water pumps need to be hooked to the power grid to function. When pumps are placed right next to a lake or river, they supply twice as much water as a well. A pump placed next to a coastline (salt water) only produces as much water as a well. Cost: $100 per pump.

Water Towers lets you store precious water so you won't have summer shortages in arid climates. Cost: $250 per tower.

Treatment plants clean and recycle your city's water, lessening seasonal shortages.

Cost: $500 per treatment plant.

Desalinization plants remove the salt from sea water. They are expensive, but sometimes necessary in beach communities with little or no other source of water. Desalinization plants, which need power to function, have internal pumps, and don't require extra water pumps. They produce approximately twice as much water as a water pump next to a river.

Cost: $1,000 per desalinization plant.

REWARDS

This button is like a surprise package. It will be ghosted and unavailable until you deserve a reward. Rewards are based on your city's population, and consist of special buildings and monuments to your mayoral prowess. When this tool is active, the cursor appears as a mayor tipping his hat.

The rewards you can strive to gain are... no, I won't tell you. You'll just have to wait and see for yourself.

ROADS

Roads is a multi-use tool. Clicking and holding on it opens a submenu that allows you to choose between five different road-related functions: placing roads and highways, and building tunnels, onramps and bus depots. When this tool is active, the cursor appears as a piece of paved road.

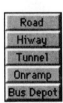

Depending on the year and technology level of your city, you may only have access to roads and tunnels. As time passes, the other options become available.

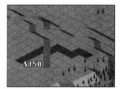

Click and drag...

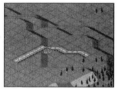

and...release.

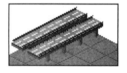

Click...

...and the Sims build the tunnel.

Road (the default setting) lets you "paint" your roads onto the land by clicking in the place where you want the road to start dragging the cursor to the place you want the road to stop, and releasing the mouse button. If you start laying a road and change your mind, you can cancel the operation by holding down the Shift key before you release the mouse button.

Roads can run in straight lines, 90-degree angles and 45-degree angles. When roads cross, they form an intersection. If you lay a road across water and it is possible to build a bridge, you will be told how much it will cost. If a bridge can't be built, you will be notified.

Cost: $10 per road tile.

Highways are high-capacity roads that are raised above the ground on pylons. They can handle four times as many cars as regular roads. They are placed the same way as roads. You will need to place onramps to allow cars to get on and off highways. When highways cross, they form cloverleafs. If you lay a highway across water and it is possible to build a bridge, you will be told how much it will cost. If a bridge can't be built, you will be notified.

Cost: $100 per highway section (4 tiles).

Tunnel lets you make pathways for roads through hills and mountains. Tunnels cannot curve, and you cannot cross tunnels, even at different altitudes. To place a tunnel, click on the tile that you want as your entrance point. The entrance point must be a sloped tile. Your highway engineers won't try to build a tunnel where it's impossible to build, or where it is unsafe, due to unstable terrain. If you pick a good spot, an engineer's report will tell you how much the tunnel will cost and ask if you want to go ahead or not.

Cost: $150 per tile of tunnel.

Engineers Report:
Unstable Terrain at Exit Point

Engineers Report:
$750
Yes   No

Onramps allow cars and buses to travel back and forth between roads and highways. Place them as junctions between roads and highways. For best results, put onramps on both sides of a highway. Cost: $25 per tile.

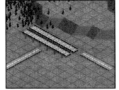

Ready for onramps   Onramps placed

Bus Depots allow commuters to take the bus to work and help alleviate traffic. They must be placed on level ground. You will need at least two bus depots since buses travel between them. Passengers can get on and off between depots.

Cost: $250 per depot.

RAILS

Rails is a multi-use tool. Clicking and holding on it opens a submenu that allows you to choose between four different rail-related functions: placing rails, placing subways (underground rails), building rail depots and building subway stations. When this tool is active, the cursor appears as a length of track.

Depending on the year and technology level of your city, you may only have access to rails and rail depots. As time passes, the other options become available.

Rail (the default setting) lets you "paint" your tracks onto the land by clicking in the place where you want the rail to start, dragging the cursor to the place where you want it to stop, and releasing the mouse button. If you start laying a rail and change your mind, you can cancel the operation by holding down the Shift key before you release the mouse button. Rails are useless without rail depots. Cost: $25 per tile.

Subways are an underground rail system. The are placed in the same way as rails, but while looking at the underground view. Subways are useless without subway stations.

Cost: $100 per tile.

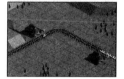

Rail Depots allow commuters to get on and off trains. Without depots, rails are useless. They must be placed on level ground, and adjacent to tracks.

Cost: $500 per depot.

Subway Stations allow passengers access to subway trains. Subway trains only stop at stations. They must be placed on level ground, adjacent to a subway line. It's usually easiest to place subway stations while looking at the underground level.

Cost: $250 per depot.

Subway Stations above ground

Subway Stations below ground

Subway to Rail Junctions allow you to hook up your subways and above-ground rails for a continuous transit system. They must be placed adjacent to a rail tile.

Cost $250 per tile.

Subway/Rail Junction above ground

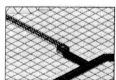

Subway/Rail Junction below ground

PORTS

Ports is a dual-purpose tool that allows you to place both airports and seaports. Click and hold on the Ports button to open a menu and choose the type of port you want to place. When this tool is active, the cursor will appear as an anchor and radar dish.

Ports are placed by clicking and dragging to form a square or rectangle, then releasing the mouse button. If you start placing a port and change your mind, you can cancel the operation by holding down the Shift key before you release the mouse button. Ports must be powered before they will develop. Seaports must be on a shoreline to be of any use.

Cost: $150 per seaport tile, $250 per airport tile.

Seaport

Airport

RESIDENTIAL ZONES

The Residential Zone tool lets you, as mayor, designate areas of your city as places where people live. Clicking and holding on Residential Zones opens a submenu that lets you choose whether the zones will be low-density (light) or high-density (dense). When this tool is active, the cursor will appear as a little house.

To zone an area as residential, click and hold on the terrain, drag the mouse, creating a rectangle, then release the mouse button. If you start laying down a zone line and change your mind, you can cancel the operation by holding down the Shift key before you release the mouse button. If you zone residential over an area that includes some tiles that are already the same density residential, you will not be charged for zoning those tiles. If you zone over an undeveloped area that is already commercial, industrial or a different density residential, it will be rezoned and you will be charged. You cannot rezone an area that is already developed.

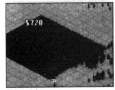

Click and drag...

...and release.

Cost: Light Residential $5 per tile, Dense Residential $10 per tile.

COMMERCIAL ZONES

The Commercial Zone tool lets you, as mayor, designate areas of your city as places where people build stores, offices and other places of commerce. Clicking and holding on Commercial Zones opens a submenu that lets you choose whether the zones will be low-density (light) or high-density (dense). When this tool is active, the cursor will appear as a little office building.

To zone an area as commercial, click and hold on the terrain, then drag the mouse, creating a rectangle, then release the mouse button. If you start laying down a zone line and change your mind, you can cancel the operation by holding down the Shift key before you release the mouse button. If you zone commercial over an area that includes some tiles that are already the same density commercial, you will not be charged for rezoning those tiles. If you zone commercial over an undeveloped area that is already residential, industrial or a different density commercial, it will be rezoned and you will be charged. You cannot rezone an area that is already developed.

Cost: Light Commercial $5 per tile, Dense Commercial $10 per tile.

INDUSTRIAL ZONES

The Industrial Zone tool lets you, as mayor, designate areas of your city as places where people build factories. Clicking and holding on Industrial Zones opens a submenu that lets you choose whether the zones will be low-density (light) or high-density (dense). When this tool is active, the cursor will appear as a little factory.

To zone an area as industrial, click and hold on the terrain, then drag the mouse, creating a rectangle, then release the mouse button. If you start placing a zone and change your mind, you can cancel the operation by holding down the Shift key before you release the mouse button. If you zone industrial over an area that includes some tiles that are already the same density industrial, you will not be charged for rezoning those tiles. If you zone industrial over an undeveloped area that is already commercial,

esidential or a different density industrial, it will be rezoned and you will be charged. You cannot rezone an area that is already developed.

Cost: Light Industrial $5 per tile, Dense Industrial $10 per tile.

EDUCATION

Education is a multi-function tool that lets you provide your citizens with everything they need to improve their minds. Click and hold on the Education button to open a submenu with the following smart choices: School, College, Library and Museum. When this tool is active, the cursor will appear as a mortarboard.

Cost: $250 per school, $1,000 per college, $500 per library, $1,000 per museum.

School   College   Library   Museum

CITY SERVICES

City Services is a multi-function tool that lets you provide your city with those necessities of life that we all wish weren't necessary. Click and hold on the City Services button to open a submenu with the following unpleasant choices: Police, Fire Station, Hospital and Prison. When this tool is active, the cursor will appear as a badge.

Cost: $500 per police station, $500 per fire station, $500 per hospital, $3,000 per prison.

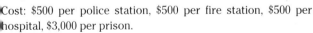

Police Station   Fire Station   Hospital   Prison

RECREATION

Recreation is a multi-function tool that lets you provide your citizens with places to have a little rest, relaxation and plain old fun. Click and hold on the Recreation button to open a submenu with the following exciting choices: Small Park, Big Park, Zoo, Stadium, Marina. When this tool is active, the cursor will appear as a bunch of balloons!

Cost: $20 per small park, $150 per big park, $3,000 per zoo, $5,000 per stadium, $1,000 per marina.

Small Park

Big Park   Zoo   Stadium   Marina

SIGNS

The Sign tool lets you label streets, buildings and points of interest in your city. When this tool is active, the cursor will appear as a little sign. To make a sign, activate the Sign tool and click on the place where you want it to appear. When the dialog box opens, type in the words you want the sign to say, then click DONE. There is no cost for placing signs.

The display of your signs can be turned on and off with the Display Signs button.

This is how most municipal planning and zoning systems are supposed to work: When meaningful changes to a city's makeup are suggested, planners select options for review and assemble reports for discussion. If these discussions become controversial, the reports are analyzed by elected (political) officials and a decision is made, in theory, based upon a thorough study of options, facts and findings.

XVII

QUERY

Query is a tool for closely inspecting different parts of your city. When this tool is active, the cursor appears as a magnifying glass. To get information, activate the tool, then click anywhere. A dialog box will open, and display fascinating facts about the spot where you clicked.

Once you have viewed the dialog box, you can *usually* just click anywhere to make it go away. Sometimes the Query dialog box allows you to rename buildings (like stadiums). In these cases, you will have to click on the DONE button to close the box. Click on RENAME if you want to change the name of the queried building. There is no cost to use the Query tool.

There is a keyboard shortcut for the Query tool—just hold down the Shift key and click anywhere in the terrain.

ROTATE COUNTER-CLOCKWISE

Click on this button to rotate the entire city limits 90 degrees counter-clockwise. There is no cost for rotating.

ROTATE CLOCKWISE

Click on this button to rotate the entire city limits 90 degrees clockwise. There is no cost for rotating.

ZOOM OUT

Click here to zoom out for a smaller, farther-out view in the City window. There are three zoom levels. If you are currently zoomed all the way out, this button will be ghosted and unavailable. There is no cost for zooming.

ZOOM IN

Click here to zoom in for an enlarged, closer view in the City window. There are three zoom levels. If you are currently zoomed all the way in, this button will be ghosted and unavailable. There is no cost for zooming.

CENTER

The Center tool lets you pick a place in your city to be centered in the City window. Just activate the tool and click anywhere in the city. When Center is active, the cursor will appear as a target sight. There is a keyboard shortcut for activating the center tool—hold down the Option key if you have one, or the Control key if you don't. There is no cost for centering.

MAP WINDOW BUTTON

The Map Window button can open the Map window in two modes: momentary and stationary. Click and hold the button to momentarily pop up a small map of the entire city limits. A rectangle somewhere in the map will outline the area of the city that is visible in the City window. The map will disappear when you release the button.

If you click the button and drag it away from the toolbar, the Map window will open (and stay there), complete with its own toolbar for different map displays. Complete information on the Map window can be found later in this section of the manual.

GRAPHS WINDOW BUTTON

The Graphs Window button can open the Graphs window in two modes: momentary and stationary. Click and hold the button to momentarily pop up a graph of city data. The graph will disappear when you release the button.

If you click the button and drag it away from the toolbar, the Graphs window will open (and stay there), complete with its own toolbar for different graph displays. Complete information on the Graphs window can be found later in this section of the manual.

POPULATION WINDOW BUTTON

The Population Window button can open the Population window in two modes: momentary and stationary. Click and hold the button to momentarily pop up a population graph. The graph will disappear when you release the button.

f you click the button and drag it away from the toolbar, the Population window will open (and stay there), complete with three buttons for different population displays. Complete information on the Population window can be found later in this section of the manual.

CITY INDUSTRY WINDOW BUTTON

The City Industry Window button can open the City Industry window in two modes: momentary and stationary. Click and hold the button to momentarily pop up an industry graph. The graph will disappear when you release the button.

f you click the button and drag it away from the toolbar, the City Industry window will open (and stay there), complete with three buttons for different industrial displays. Complete information on the City Industry window can be found later in this section of the manual.

NEIGHBORS WINDOW BUTTON

The Neighbors Window button can open the Neighbors window in two modes: momentary and stationary. Click and hold the button to momentarily pop up a display of your city and its neighboring cities, with their individual and collective populations. The display will disappear when you release the button.

If you click the button and drag it away from the toolbar, the Neighbors window will open (and stay there). Complete information on the Neighbors window can be found later in this section of the manual.

BUDGET WINDOW BUTTON

Click here to open the Budget window. (There is no momentary view.) Complete information on the Budget window can be found later in this section of the manual.

SHOW BUILDINGS

Click here to toggle on and off the display of all buildings in the City window. The buildings won't really go away—they'll just be invisible until you turn them back on.

SHOW SIGNS

Click here to toggle on and off the display of all signs in the City window. The signs will be invisible until you turn them back on.

SHOW INFRASTRUCTURE

Click here to toggle on and off the display of all miscellaneous city infrastructure items in the City window (roads, rails, subway lines, power lines, water pumps and subway stations).

SHOW ZONES

This button works differently depending on whether you're looking at the normal or underground view. In the normal view, clicking here toggles on and off the display of all buildings in zones. It doesn't affect city-owned buildings like police and fire stations, educational facilities, depots or power plants, but does include ports and military bases. In underground view, it toggles on and off a color display that lets you know where your zones are without jumping back upstairs.

SHOW UNDERGROUND

Click here to toggle between the surface and the underground displays.

HELP

Click here for a friendly reminder that you can get help on each of these buttons by holding down the Shift key and clicking on the button in question.

DEMAND INDICATOR

The Demand Indicator gives you a constant readout of what types of zones the Sims in your city need. Depending on the size of your city, the indicator can take up to a few minutes to respond to your changes, so be patient.

THE TERRAIN TOOLBAR

When the City window is in terrain-editing mode, it has the Terrain toolbar—your control center for modifying and customizing landscapes. It can be moved around your screen by clicking and dragging the bar at the top. There is no charge for any terrain modifications in terrain-editing mode. All the tools in the Terrain toolbar are explained below.

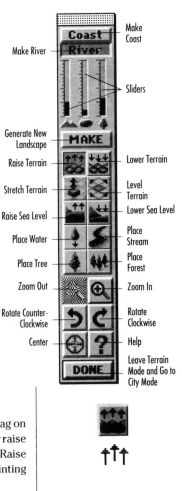

Make Coast
Make River
Sliders
Generate New Landscape
Raise Terrain — Lower Terrain
Stretch Terrain — Level Terrain
Raise Sea Level — Lower Sea Level
Place Water — Place Stream
Place Tree — Place Forest
Zoom Out — Zoom In
Rotate Counter-Clockwise — Rotate Clockwise
Center — Help
Leave Terrain Mode and Go to City Mode

COAST

The Coast button, when depressed, creates a coastline along one side of the next landscape that is generated.

RIVER

The River button, when depressed, creates a river through the next landscape that is generated.

MOUNTAIN, WATER AND TREE SLIDERS

These sliders let you adjust the amount of the surface of your city that is covered by mountains, water and trees. Click and drag the slider bars to the levels you want. The higher the sliders, the more mountains, water or trees you get. The lower the sliders, the less you get.

MAKE

Click here to generate a new landscape based on the Coast button, the River button and the three sliders.

RAISE TERRAIN

Click on the Raise Terrain button, then click or click and drag on the terrain to raise the land. Clicking on water will eventually raise the waterbed above sea level and turn it into dry land. When Raise Terrain is active, the cursor appears as three upward-pointing arrows.

LOWER TERRAIN

Click on the Lower Terrain button, then click or click and drag on the terrain to lower the land. Clicking on dry land will eventually lower it below sea level and turn it into a lake or stream. When

Lower Terrain is active, the cursor will appear as three downward-pointing arrows.

STRETCH TERRAIN

The Stretch Terrain button lets you grab the land and stretch it up or down. Just click and hold on the terrain, then drag it either up or down. When Stretch Terrain is active, the cursor will appear as an up-and-down-pointing arrow.

LEVEL TERRAIN

The Level Terrain button lets you pick an altitude and quickly bring the land around it either up or down to match your chosen level. Just click and hold at the altitude you want, then drag the cursor around the area you want leveled. When Level Terrain is active, the cursor will appear as a flat, four-way arrow.

RAISE SEA LEVEL

Click here to raise the sea level in the terrain by one tile.

LOWER SEA LEVEL

Click here to lower the sea level in the terrain by one tile.

PLACE WATER

The Place Water tool lets you create lakes and streams by clicking where you want your water to appear. When this tool is active, the cursor appears as a water droplet.

PLACE STREAM

The Place Stream tool lets you send streams flowing down slopes into the valleys below. Click where you want the stream to begin. When this tool is active, the cursor appears as a babbling brook.

PLACE TREE

The Place Tree tool lets you add trees to the landscape. When active, the cursor will appear as a tree. Each click will place either one or two trees. Click repeatedly on a single tile to create dense thickets, and click and drag across many tiles to create forests. Hold down the Shift key while using Place Tree to remove trees

PLACE FOREST

The Place Forest tool works like Place Tree, except it places trees on a number of tiles with each click. When active, the cursor will appear as a tiny little forest. Hold down the Shift key while using Place Forest to remove forests.

ZOOM OUT

Click here to zoom out for a smaller, farther-out view in the City window. There are three zoom levels. If you are currently zoomed all the way out, this button will be ghosted and unavailable.

ZOOM IN

Click here to zoom in for an enlarged, closer view in the City window. There are three zoom levels. If you are currently zoomed all the way in, this button will be ghosted and unavailable.

ROTATE COUNTER-CLOCKWISE

Click here to rotate the entire city limits 90 degrees counter-clockwise.

ROTATE CLOCKWISE

Click here to rotate the entire city limits 90 degrees clockwise.

CENTER

The Center tool lets you pick a place in your city to be centered in the City window. Just activate the tool and click anywhere in the city. There is a keyboard shortcut for activating the Center tool—hold down the Option key if you have one, or the Control key if you don't. When Center is active, the cursor appears as a target sight.

HELP

Click here for a friendly reminder that you can get help on each of these buttons by holding down the Shift key and clicking on the button in question.

DONE

Click here when you are done editing the terrain and are ready to switch over to city-building mode.

Map Window

IN GENERAL

The Map window shows your complete city limits at once with vital information in a number of different map displays. It can be opened by selecting Map from the Windows menu. It can also be opened—in two ways—with the Map button on the City toolbar.

Close Box Title Bar Zoom Box

Map Toolbar

City Window Rectangle

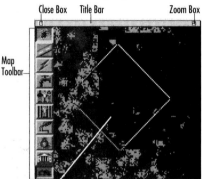

If you click and hold on the Map button, the map (just the map—no Title bar or frame) will pop up, and then go away when you release the button. If you click and drag the button, the full Map window will appear.

The Map window can be moved around the screen by clicking and dragging the Title bar. It can be closed by clicking the Close box.

The Map window has two sizes. Click the Zoom box to toggle between the two sizes. This may vary on different computers; check your machine-specific Addendum.

All map displays include the terrain. Trees and forests are green, water is blue and the land is different shades of brown—the higher the altitude, the lighter the shade.

Somewhere in the map is a rectangle that outlines the area of the city that currently shows in the City window. Clicking on the map moves the rectangle to the place where you clicked, then redraws the City window to show the rectangle's new contents.

THE MAP TOOLBAR

The Map toolbar has a number of buttons that let you see a number of different map displays. The pop-up map, which has no toolbar, always shows the last-selected display. Some of the buttons on the toolbar have submenus for even more displays. In maps that display information in shades of grey, the darker the grey, the higher, heavier or denser the item being mapped.

CITY FORM

The City Form button controls two map displays. Click and hold on it to open a submenu that lets you choose between displaying structures and zones.

Structures shows buildings and city infrastructure, including roads, rails, etc. Zones shows the areas that have been zoned. Residential zones are shown green, commercial zones are blue and industrial zones are yellow.

ROADS

The Roads button controls three map displays. Click and hold on it to open a submenu that lets you choose between displaying roads, rails and traffic density.

Roads and Rails show the transportation pathways in your city. Traffic density shows the relative amount of traffic in different parts of the city in shades of grey.

POWER GRID

The Power Grid button activates a display of the power grid in your city. Powered zones are shown in yellow, zones that have lost power are shown in red, and power lines are shown in white.

WATER SYSTEM

The Water System button activates a display of the water grid in your city. Zones that are hooked to the water supply are shown in yellow, zones that have no water are shown in red, and water pipes are shown in white.

POPULATION

The Population button controls two map displays. Click and hold on it to open a submenu that lets you choose between displaying population density and the rate of population growth.

Population Density shows the relative number of Sims in each part of your city in shades of grey. Rate of Growth shows where in the city the population is increasing in shades of blue, and where it is decreasing in shades of red. The darker the blue or red, the more drastic the population change.

CRIME

The Crime button controls three map displays. Click and hold on it to open a submenu that lets you choose between displaying crime rate, police power, and police department location.

Crime Rate shows the relative amount of crime in each area of your city in shades of grey. Police Power shows the relative amount of police coverage in different areas of the city, also in shades of grey. Police Departments shows each of your stations as a white square.

POLLUTION

The Pollution button activates a display of the relative amounts of pollution in your city. This is a reading of all types of pollution combined, and is shown in shades of grey.

LAND VALUE

The Land Value button activates a display of the relative property values in the city, shown in shades of grey.

CITY SERVICES

The City Services button controls four map displays. Click and hold on it to open a submenu that lets you choose between displaying fire department power, fire department location, schools and colleges.

Fire Power shows the relative fire coverage of different parts of your city in shades of grey. Fire Departments, Schools and Colleges show the locations of these buildings as white squares.

MAP MODE BUTTON

This button toggles the City window between its current mode and Map mode. In Map mode the terrain in the City window displays the same information as the Map window. You can return the City window to its previous mode by either clicking the Map Mode button again or closing the Map window.

The Budget window reports and lets you adjust your city's budget. It automatically opens every January, unless Auto-Budget (in the Options menu) is on. It can also be opened manually by selecting Budget in the Windows menu, or by clicking on the Budget window button in the City toolbar.

Budget Window

The Budget window closes automatically all by itself after about two minutes. The two-minute timer is reset whenever you click on the window. You can close it any time you want by clicking on the Done button.

The upper-left corner of the Budget window displays your city's name, the current year and month, and the timer.

Click the Help button for a friendly reminder that you can get help on each area, item and button in this window by holding down the Shift key and clicking.

		2037 To Date Expense	2037 Year End Estimate		
Itty Bitty City 2037 Budget June 2037				Done	Help
Property Taxes	%5	1749	4202		
City Ordinances		346	833		
Bond Payments		0	0		
Police Department	%100	-875	-2100		
Fire Department	%100	-250	-600		
Health & Welfare	%100	-208	-500		
Education	%100	-103	-250		
Transit Authority	%100	-135	-326		
Year to Date Cashflow$		$522			
Estimated Annual Cashflow$			$1,259		
Current Funds$			$125,835		
End of Year Funds$			$127,094		

THE NUMBERS

The Budget window has eight rows of figures that cover all the city's revenues and expenses. Below those figures is a summary of the current financial situation and an estimate of what your finances will be at the end of the year.

Each revenue or expense has:

- The name of the revenue or expense. Shift-click on the name to bring up a helpful explanation of what it is and what it does.

- A percentage setting (in most cases) where you set either the tax rate you are charging or the amount of funding you are allotting.

- A year-to-date figure showing the up-to-the-moment amount that you've spent or made.

- An annual estimate of what you will have spent or made at the end of the year at the current budget settings.

- Detailed books showing a monthly breakdown of the revenue or expense. In some cases the book dialog just shows information, but some of the books also allow access to other, more detailed budgeting functions.

- An advisor who reports current status and/or gives suggestions about what you should do.

Note: When the Budget window opens automatically at the beginning of a new year, the Year-to-Date column shows the total for the year that just ended and the Annual Estimate column shows estimated costs for the year that is just beginning.

Below is a detailed explanation of each budget item.

PROPERTY TAXES

Property taxes are your main source of cash for maintaining and expanding your city. You can set the overall tax rate for all zones by clicking on the up- and down-arrows. The minimum tax is 0%, the maximum is 20%. Any taxes you set here will be equally applied to all zones. You can independently set the tax rates for residential, commercial and industrial zones in the Property Taxes Books.

Clicking on the Books icon displays a detailed report of the year's past and projected tax income. For each month, the following information is given:

- The residential zone tax rate and tax amount

- The commercial zone tax rate and tax amount

- The industrial zone tax rate and tax amount
- A running total of the taxes that will come due at the end of the year

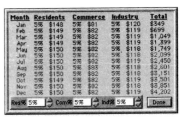

Month	Residents		Commerce		Industry		Total
Jan	5%	$148	5%	$81	5%	$120	$349
Feb	5%	$149	5%	$82	5%	$119	$699
Mar	5%	$149	5%	$82	5%	$119	$1,049
Apr	5%	$149	5%	$82	5%	$119	$1,399
May	5%	$150	5%	$82	5%	$118	$1,749
Jun	5%	$150	5%	$82	5%	$118	$2,099
Jul	5%	$150	5%	$82	5%	$119	$2,450
Aug	5%	$150	5%	$83	5%	$118	$2,601
Sep	5%	$150	5%	$82	5%	$118	$3,151
Oct	5%	$149	5%	$82	5%	$119	$3,501
Nov	5%	$150	5%	$82	5%	$118	$3,851
Dec	5%	$150	5%	$82	5%	$119	$4,202

Res% 5%   Com% 5%   Ind% 5%   Done

At the bottom of the dialog box, you can set individual tax rates for the three types of zones. If you change the tax rates here, the overall rate as shown in the Budget window will display the average of the three rates.

Click on Done to close the Property Taxes Books.

CITY ORDINANCES

This line item is a summary of the costs and revenues of all combined city ordinances. These range from education drives to sales taxes to neighborhood watch to an annual carnival.

Usually, you, as mayor, must approve and establish these programs, but if your city is doing very well, the City Council may take it upon itself to enact some programs that benefit the city. These programs are viewed and established in the Ordinance window, which can opened from the Budget window by clicking on the Community Programs Book icon. The Ordinance window will be described in detail below.

Finance			Safety & Health		
1% Sales Tax	✓	196	Volunteer Fire Dept.	✓	-120
1% Income Tax	✓	360	Public Smoking Ban		
Legalized Gambling	✓	98	Free Clinics	✓	-180
Parking Fines	✓	180	Junior Sports		

Education			Promotional		
Pro-Reading Campaign	✓	-60	Tourist Advertising	✓	-196
Anti-Drug Campaign			Business Advertising		
CPR Training	✓	-60	City Beautification		
Neighborhood Watch			Annual Carnival	✓	-65

Other			Estimated Annual Cost	
Energy Conservation	✓	0	Finance	$835
Nuclear Free Zone			Safety & Health	-$300
Homeless Shelters			Education	-$120
Pollution Controls	✓	-142	Promotional	-$262
			Other	-$142

Done   YTD Total $346   EST Total $352

Click Done to return to the Budget window.

BOND PAYMENTS

This is the interest you pay on bond issues.

If you need cash above and beyond the money you make from property taxes, you can issue municipal bonds, which is basically a loan from your citizens. All bonds are issued for $10,000. The interest you pay on outstanding bonds is prime rate plus 1%, plus an additional percentage based on your city's current value and loan rating.

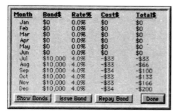

Month	Bond$	Rate%	Cost$	Total$
Jan	$0	0.0%	$0	$0
Feb	$0	0.0%	$0	$0
Mar	$0	0.0%	$0	$0
Apr	$0	0.0%	$0	$0
May	$0	0.0%	$0	$0
Jun	$0	0.0%	$0	$0
Jul	$10,000	4.0%	-$33	-$33
Aug	$10,000	4.0%	-$33	-$66
Sep	$10,000	4.0%	-$34	-$100
Oct	$10,000	4.0%	-$33	-$133
Nov	$10,000	4.0%	-$33	-$166
Dec	$10,000	4.0%	-$34	-$200

[Show Bonds] [Issue Bond] [Repay Bond] [Done]

Clicking on the Interest book icon opens a dialog box with detailed information and buttons for extra financial transactions.

For each month of the year, the following information is given: (actual amounts are shown in blue, projected amounts are shown in red.)

- The bonds you have outstanding
- The average interest rate you pay on the bonds
- The monthly amount of interest you pay on the bonds
- The accumulated total interest paid

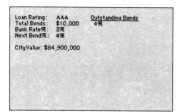

Loan Rating:	AAA	Outstanding Bonds
Total Bonds:	$10,000	4%
Bank Rate%:	3%	
Next Bond%:	4%	
City Value: $84,900,000		

Show Bonds displays:

- Your city's current loan rating
- The total number of bonds you have outstanding
- The current interest rate the bank is paying on your account
- The interest rate you will pay on a bond if you issue it now
- The current value of your city (the infrastructure)

Loan ratings range from AAA to F. Your rating is based on your city value. The higher your rating, the more bonds you can issue and the lower the interest rate you pay on them.

Issue Bond opens a dialog that tells you the current interest rate for bonds and asks you if you want to issue one. All bonds are $10,000. If you need or want more than $10,000, then you can issue two bonds. If you need or want less, too bad—take the $10,000 and keep what you don't spend in the bank. If your loan rating or city value is too low, you won't be allowed to issue any more bonds.

Current Rates are 4%
Do You Want to Issue the Bond?
[Yes]   [No]

Oldest Bond Rate is 4%
Do You Want to Repay the Bond?
[Yes]   [No]

Repay Bond opens a dialog that tells you the interest rate on the oldest outstanding bond, and asks if you want to repay it. Bonds are always repaid from the oldest to the newest. During the life of the bond, interest accrues monthly, and is paid out at the end of

each year from your city funds. You will pay the interest every year until you repay the bond, so once you're flush with cash, pay them off and get out of debt.

Clicking on Done closes the book.

POLICE DEPARTMENT

This is the cost and funding level for police departments in your city. You can set the percentage of funding for your departments by clicking on the up- and down-arrows. In general, try to keep police funding as high as possible to prevent rampant crime. Any funding you set will be equally distributed to all police departments. Complete funding for a police station is $100 per year.

Clicking on the Books icon displays a detailed report of the year's past and projected police funding costs. For each month, the following information is given:

Month	Police	Fund	Cost	Total
Jan	21	100%	-$175	-$175
Feb	21	100%	-$175	-$350
Mar	21	100%	-$175	-$525
Apr	21	100%	-$175	-$700
May	21	100%	-$175	-$875
Jun	21	100%	-$175	-$1,050
Jul	21	100%	-$175	-$1,225
Aug	21	100%	-$175	-$1,400
Sep	21	100%	-$175	-$1,575
Oct	21	100%	-$175	-$1,750
Nov	21	100%	-$175	-$1,925
Dec	21	100%	-$175	-$2,100

- The number of police stations in the city
- The funding level you have set
- The actual monthly cost to fund your stations
- A running total of the yearly cost

There are no additional buttons or functions here, so just click anywhere to close the books.

FIRE DEPARTMENT

This is the cost and funding level for fire departments in your city. You can set the percentage of funding for your departments by clicking on the up- and down-arrows. In general, try to keep fire funding as high as possible for both preventing fires and responding to emergencies. Any funding you set will be equally distributed to all fire departments. A fully funded fire station costs $100 per year.

Clicking on the Books icon displays a detailed report of the year's past and projected fire funding costs. For each month, the following information is given:

- The number of fire stations in the city
- The funding level you have set
- The actual monthly cost to fund your stations
- A running total of the yearly cost

Month	Fire Dept	Fund	Cost	Total
Jan	6	100%	-$50	-$50
Feb	6	100%	-$50	-$100
Mar	6	100%	-$50	-$150
Apr	6	100%	-$50	-$200
May	6	100%	-$50	-$250
Jun	6	100%	-$50	-$300
Jul	6	100%	-$50	-$350
Aug	6	100%	-$50	-$400
Sep	6	100%	-$50	-$450
Oct	6	100%	-$50	-$500
Nov	6	100%	-$50	-$550
Dec	6	100%	-$50	-$600

There are no additional buttons or functions here, so just click anywhere to close the books.

HEALTH & WELFARE

This is the cost and funding level for medical services in your city. You can set the percentage of funding for your hospitals by clicking on the up- and down-arrows. In general, try to keep funding as high as possible to keep your Sims healthy. If you keep your funding at 100% for several decades, the average life expectancy in your city will increase. Any funding you set will be equally distributed to all hospitals. Complete funding for a hospital is $75 per year.

Month	Hospital	Fund	Cost	Total
Jan	5	100%	-$41	-$41
Feb	5	100%	-$42	-$83
Mar	5	100%	-$42	-$125
Apr	5	100%	-$41	-$166
May	5	100%	-$42	-$208
Jun	5	100%	-$42	-$250
Jul	5	100%	-$41	-$291
Aug	5	100%	-$42	-$333
Sep	5	100%	-$42	-$375
Oct	5	100%	-$41	-$416
Nov	5	100%	-$42	-$458
Dec	5	100%	-$42	-$500

Clicking on the Books icon displays a detailed report of the year's past and projected medical funding costs. For each month, the following information is given:

- The number of hospitals in the city
- The funding level you have set
- The actual monthly cost to fund your hospitals
- A running total of the yearly cost

There are no additional buttons or functions here, so just click anywhere to close the books.

EDUCATION

This is the cost and funding level for education in your city. This funding supports both schools for the children and colleges for higher learning. Without schools, education in your city will be entirely based on verbal lore, and you will be unable to support high-technology industries.

You can set the percentage of funding for education by clicking on the up- and down-arrows. Any funding you set here will be equally distributed to all schools and colleges. You can independently set the funding rates for schools and colleges in the Education books. Complete funding for a school costs $25 per year, and a college costs $100 per year.

Clicking on the Books icon displays a detailed report of the year's past and projected education funding. For each month, the following information is given:

- The number of schools in the city
- The funding level for schools
- The monthly cost to fund schools
- The number of colleges in the city
- The funding level for colleges
- The monthly cost to fund colleges
- A running total of the yearly cost

At the bottom of the dialog box, you can set individual funding levels for schools and colleges. If you change the funding levels here, the overall level as shown in the Budget window will display the average of school and college funding levels.

Click on Done to close the Education books.

TRANSIT AUTHORITY

This is the cost and funding level for maintaining the transportation system in your city. This funding maintains roads, rails highways, subways, bridges and tunnels. Without proper funding, your transit systems will deteriorate and commuting and commerce in your city will fall to pieces.

You can set the overall percentage of funding for your transportation systems by clicking on the up- and down-arrows. Any funding you set here will be equally distributed to all types of transportation. You can independently set the funding rates for roads, rails, highways, subways, bridges and tunnels in the Transit Authority Books. Complete transit authority funding per year is: Roads $1 per 10 tiles; Rails $1 per 5 tiles; Highways $1 per section (4 tiles); Subways $2 per 5 tiles; Bridges $2 per 5 tiles; Tunnels $2 per 5 tiles.

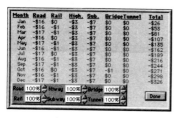

Clicking on the Books icon displays a detailed report of the year's past and projected transit authority funding. For each month, the following information is given:

- The cost of road maintenance
- The cost of rail maintenance
- The cost of highway maintenance
- The cost of subway maintenance
- The cost of bridge maintenance
- The cost of tunnel maintenance
- A running total of all transit costs

At the bottom of the dialog box, you can set individual funding levels for roads, rails, highways, subways, bridges and tunnels. If you change the funding levels here, the overall level as shown in the Budget window will display the average of all these funding levels.

Click on Done to close the Transit Authority Books.

THE TOTALS

The bottom of the Budget window shows the totals for:

- Year-to-Date Cash Flow
- Estimated Annual Cash Flow
- Current Funds
- (Estimated) End of Year Funds

The Ordinance window is where community programs and city ordinances are established and inspected. This window can be opened either by selecting Ordinance from the Windows menu or by clicking on the City Ordinance Book icon in the Budget window.

There are five categories of programs and ordinances: finance, health and safety, education, promotional and other. Click on the names of each program or ordinance for an explanation of what they do as well as their pros and cons.

To enact a program, click in the checkbox to the right of the program's name. The cost or projected revenue will appear to the right of the check. These amounts will vary with the size and development of your city. The Estimated Annual Costs for all programs is provided in the lower-right corner of the window.

Click Done to close the Ordinance window.

Ordinance Window

Finance		
1% Sales Tax	✓	196
1% Income Tax	✓	360
Legalized Gambling	✓	98
Parking Fines	✓	180

Safety & Health		
Volunteer Fire Dept.	✓	-120
Public Smoking Ban		
Free Clinics	✓	-180
Junior Sports		

Education		
Pro-Reading Campaign	✓	-60
Anti-Drug Campaign		
CPR Training	✓	-60
Neighborhood Watch		

Promotional		
Tourist Advertising	✓	-196
Business Advertising		
City Beautification		
Annual Carnival	✓	-65

Other		
Energy Conservation	✓	0
Nuclear Free Zone		
Homeless Shelters		
Pollution Controls	✓	-142

Estimated Annual Cost	
Finance	$835
Safety & Health	-$300
Education	-$120
Promotional	-$262
Other	-$142

Done	YTD Total$ 346	EST Total$ 352

FINANCE PROGRAMS

1% Sales Tax will add cash to your coffers, but may also inhibit local commerce.

1% Income Tax is a source of city revenues, but may discourage residential growth, and even cause some tax-haters to move away.

Legalized Gambling can provide extra money that can be put t[o] good use, but brings with it an increase in crime.

Parking Fines are a small, steady source of the green, but tend t[o] hinder commercial growth a little.

SAFETY & HEALTH PROGRAMS

A Volunteer Fire Department can be an economical way to figh[t] fires in small communities, but can't replace the professionals i[n] a big city or during a forest fire.

A Public Smoking Ban can increase the overall health level in you[r] city and eventually increase the average life expectancy, but wil[l] cost a small fee to administer.

Free Clinics increase the overall health level in the city, but fre[e] clinics aren't free—at least not to you.

Junior Sports increases the overall health level of the youth o[f] your city.

EDUCATION PROGRAMS

A Pro-Reading Campaign will increase the overall education leve[l] in your city, preparing it for an influx of new, high-tech industries[.]

An Anti-Drug Campaign can help reduce crime.

Providing CPR Training as a service to your Sims increases the overall level of health in your city.

Neighborhood Watch helps reduce crime in residential areas, but at a price.

PROMOTIONAL PROGRAMS

Tourism Advertising may or may not pay off in bringing visitors[,] with their loose dollars to your fair city. If you do advertise for

tourists, make sure you have the right attractions, like marinas, stadiums, parks, zoos, rivers, etc.

Business Advertising can bring new industry into town, but make sure you can support the businesses with ample water, power, transportation, and enough residential and commercial space to hold the influx of new citizens. And low taxes won't hurt, either.

City Beautification increases residential desirability and land value.

An Annual Carnival can increase tourist trade and local commerce, and show your Sims a darn good time. The size, cost and benefit of the carnival varies with your city size.

OTHER PROGRAMS

Energy Conservation establishes an educational drive to conserve electricity by, among other things, adding insulation to homes and water heaters. This program takes a few years to ramp up to full effect, but will eventually allow your power plants to power up to 15% more buildings.

Declaring your city a Nuclear Free Zone costs nothing, but can make some of your citizens feel safer, and may even attract new citizens to your fair town. It's a small plus for residential desirability and a small minus for industry. A Nuclear Free Zone will not stop the military from building missile silos or basing nuclear weapons near your city if you give them permission to build a base.

Homeless Shelters are expensive, but decrease the number of homeless people and increase the number of residents, increasing the labor pool for commerce and industry and marginally increasing land value.

Pollution Controls slightly lower the amount of industrial pollution in your city, but also make the city slightly less desirable to industry.

ESTIMATED ANNUAL COST

This section of the Ordinance window summarizes the cost o income from each category, and gives both year-to-date and full year estimated totals.

Population Window

The Population window displays graphs of statistics about you city's population. It can be opened by selecting Population from the Windows menu. It can also be opened—in two ways—with the Population button on the City toolbar.

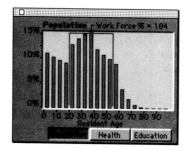

If you click and hold on the Population button, the population graph (just the graph—no Title bar or frame) will pop up, and then go away when you release the button. If you click and drag the button, the full Population window wil appear, complete with buttons for additional displays.

The Population window can be moved around the screen by clicking and dragging the Title bar. It can be closed by clicking the Close box. The three buttons on the bottom of the window let you choose between three different population-related graphic displays:

Population shows the age distribution of your population, and gives the percentage of the population that is your potential work force.

Health shows the Life Expectancy (LE) of your population, by age, and summarizes the LE of your work force.

Education shows the average education level of your citizens at various ages, expressed in their Education Quotient (EQ). A high EQ attracts high-tech industry to your city. EQ is affected by the presence of schools, colleges, libraries and museums.

Industries Window

The Industries window displays graphs of statistics about your city's industry. It can be opened by selecting Industry from the Windows menu. It can also be opened—in two ways—with the Industry button on the City toolbar.

If you click and hold on the Industry button, the industry graph (just the graph—no Title bar or frame) will pop up, and then go away when you release the button. If you click and drag the button, the full Industries window will appear, complete with buttons for additional displays.

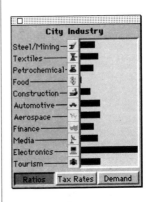

The Industries window can be moved around the screen by clicking and dragging the Title bar. It can be closed by clicking the Close box. The three buttons on the bottom of the window let you choose between three different industry-related graphic displays:

Ratios shows the distribution of various types of industries in your city.

Tax Rates shows the rate at which various industries are taxed. This is the property tax for industry as set in the Budget window. You can change the rate for individual industries by dragging the blue bar to the right (increase tax) or left (decrease tax). You may want to lower taxes on an industry to encourage its growth within your city. You may want to increase taxes to discourage an industry, or to fine it for causing excess pollution.

Demand shows a graph of which industries' products are in demand nationally.

The first step of planning, the selection of options for review, is the most critical and often the most difficult procedure in this process: rarely is this done well and thoroughly. Which options are to be examined depends upon the training, intelligence, education, experience and personal biases of the person or committee selecting options.

XVIII

Graphs Window

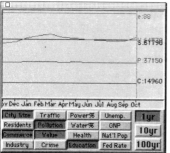

The Graphs window displays statistical graphs about many elements of your city. It can be opened by selecting Graphs from the Windows menu. It can also be opened—in two ways—with the Graphs button on the City toolbar.

If you click and hold on the Graphs button, the graph (just the graph—no Title bar or frame) will pop up, and then go away when you release the button. If you click and drag the button, the full Graphs window will appear, complete with buttons for controlling the graphs displayed.

The Graphs window can be moved around the screen by clicking and dragging the Title bar. It can be closed by clicking the Close box. The many buttons on the bottom of the window let you toggle on and off various graphic displays. Click on the 1 year, 10 year or 100 year button to set the time scale for the graphs.

Each graph:

- Is shown in a different color
- Has a "marker" letter or symbol at its right end to help you identify it
- Is followed by a number that gives its current value

City Size, marked with an "S," is the total city population.

Residents, marked with an "R," shows the population that isn't part of the job market, including children, elderly and spouses not employed outside of the home.

Commerce, marked with a "C," shows the number of people employed in commercial jobs.

Industry, marked with an "I," shows the number of people employed in industrial jobs.

Traffic, marked with a "T," shows the average density of your road network including buses, but not trains or subways. For this graph, traffic is considered road congestion, not the total amount of travel.

Pollution, marked with a "P," shows the growth or decline in the general level of pollution in the city.

Value, marked with a "V," shows the fluctuations of the average land value in the city by graphing the median home price.

Crime, marked with an "X," shows the changing crime rate in your city.

Power%, marked with a "p," shows the remaining capacity of your power plant(s). When you get to 0 you'll start to have brownouts.

Water%, marked with a "w," shows the remaining capacity of your water system. When you get to 0 you'll need more wells and pumps.

Health, marked with an "h," shows the growth or decline of the overall health level of the citizens of your city.

Education, marked with an "e," shows the ever-changing average level of education that the citizens of your city have reached.

Unemployment (Unemp.), marked with a "u," shows the changing number of people that are out of work in your city.

Gross National Product (GNP), marked with a "g," shows the total value of goods and services produced by the residents of SimNation. This affects the market for industrial goods produced in your city.

National Population (Nat'l Pop), marked with an "n," shows the changes in SimNation's total population.

Fed Rate, marked with "%," is the prime interest rate as set by SimNation's Federal Reserve Board.

SIM CITY 2000

Neighbors Window

The Neighbors window displays your city's population along with the population of its neighboring cities and the total population of SimNation. Use this window to compare your city with the cities that you compete with for people and other resources, and to see just how big a part of the whole nation you are (or aren't).

The Neighbors window can be opened by selecting Neighbors from the Windows menu. It can also be opened—in two ways—with the Neighbors button on the City toolbar.

If you click and hold on the Neighbors button, the window, with no Title bar or frame, will pop up, and then go away when you release the button. If you click and drag the button, the full Neighbors window will appear, and stay until you make it go away by clicking in the Close box.

You can move the window around on the screen by clicking and dragging the Title bar.

City planning in the United States has most often used economic and technological (scientific) variables to drive decisions regarding its municipalities. It is interesting to wonder how our new communities might develop if we based decisions on the answers to questions like:

"What is it you are trying to achieve in a human community?" and "What does this natural landscape and topography suggest is the most appropriate use of this environment?"   XIX

Whenever you start a new city, you have the choice of three difficulty levels, easy, medium and hard. The differences between the levels are:

The amount of money you start with. In an easy game, you start with $20,000. A medium game gives you $10,000. In a hard game, you start $10,000 in debt, with a bond issue to pay back when you can and interest to pay every year.

The national financial model. Your city is located somewhere in SimNation. The growth of your city depends on its surroundings—rich, financially healthy neighbors are good customers for your industrial products and, bring their money with them when they visit your tourist attractions. In easy games, SimNation is in a boom cycle. In medium games, the national economy is stable. For hard games, SimNation is in a recession.

The external industrial product demand. The easier the game, the more demand for the products that your city's industries can produce.

The propensity for disaster. The harder the game, the more likely is it that your city will be host to a disaster. Choosing No Disasters in the Disasters menu prevents disasters at all difficulty levels.

The Effect of Time

When you start a new city, you can choose between 1900, 1950, 2000 and 2050 for its founding year. And as time goes by, things change, including:

The available technology. The technology levels in SimCity 2000 roughly follow reality, give or take a few years. (Except for the future stuff, which is just guessing, so don't come to us in 2050 and complain that we don't have fusion power yet.) Inventions that give you access to new technology are announced in newspaper headlines.

The national financial model. Since the national and world population is larger now than it was in 1900, there are more potential citizens and more potential customers. External demand increases with time. It is easier to build a bigger city in 2000 than it is in 1900.

The per capita (per zone) power consumption. In 1900 there aren't many ways for the average citizen to squander energy. Then, starting around 1930, with the advent of muscle cars and electric-powered everything and lots of electronic toys, power consumption zooms, peaking around 1970. From 1970 to 2000, because of both conservation practices and more efficient gadgetry, per capita power use sinks and levels off. This energy effect in SimCity 2000 is subtle, but can be affected by passing the energy conservation ordinance in the Ordinance window.

Scenarios

SimCity 2000 scenarios are special cities with problems, included both to provide a number of gaming challenges and to help you better design your own cities by seeing the mistakes and problems other cities have faced.

Scenario cities are all in separate files, and are read into the game when you load them. Additional scenarios can be added later.

Each Scenario includes:
- A pre-built city
- A problem to solve or disaster to face
- A goal to reach
- A time limit to reach the goal

If you reach the goal within the time limit, you win the scenario, you're given the key to the city, and you can continue to rule the city. If you don't reach the goal within the time limit, you're kicked out of town.

Typical goals include:

- Reaching a population level
- Reaching a financial goal
- Rebuilding your industry
- Reducing crime, pollution or traffic

One of your primary functions as city planner is zoning—deciding what types of buildings go where. Good zoning allows all city functions to be accessed by all citizens, and sets the feel and flow of life in the city. All zones in SimCity 2000 can be decreed to be either light-density (low population) or dense (high population).

As you zone areas, the empty zones are shown in colors so you can easily keep track of them. You can turn on and off the display of empty zones in the underground view with the Show Zones button in the City toolbar.

There are three basic zones in SimCity 2000: residential, commercial and industrial.

- Residential zones, shown in green, are places where Sims live. They include everything from luxury homes to slums.
- Commercial zones, shown in blue, are the shops, stores and offices of the city.
- Industrial zones, shown in yellow, are the factories and manufacturing centers of the city.

Zones can be almost any shape or size that can be made out of squares or rectangles. If you zone over an area that is already zoned, you will be charged for rezoning only if you change the type of zone or the density. You won't be charged for zoning light residential over an existing light residential area, but you will be charged if you zone dense residential (or light or dense industrial or commercial) over light residential.

To remove zoning from an area without rezoning, use the De-zone function of the Bulldozer tool in the City toolbar.

Sims only build in zoned areas. You, as mayor, can build elements of the city infrastructure (roads, rails, power lines, power plants, etc.), city services (police and fire stations, etc.) and other public places (parks, zoos, museums, libraries, schools, etc.) either in zoned or unzoned areas.

Zones grow and decay as Sims move in and out of individual buildings, zones or the city. Depending on the times, the economy and your design skills, booming, bustling zones may be abandoned, or empty zones may suddenly become prime real estate and suddenly grow into a city center.

Specialized Zones

Seaports and airports are actually special-purpose zones. They are placed and sized like the basic (residential, commercial and industrial) zones and they needn't be placed in existing zones. Military bases are also specialized zones, but they are automatically placed by the simulation.

Non-Zones

Roads, rails, stations, depots, and city-owned buildings like power plants and police stations don't need to be placed in zones. In fact, when you place them in a zone, they de-zone that land. For example, if you place a road across a zone, then remove it with a bulldozer, the newly exposed land will be unzoned. You can save a lot of zoning money by leaving spaces between them for roads and rails and keeping your power plants, stations, depots and departments out of zoned areas.

Commerce

Commerce is primarily trade within your city. It is slow in a small city, since your internal market is small. Commerce remains a much less important aspect of a city until it reaches a population of about 100,000, where income from commerce catches up with industry. As your population grows beyond that, your city may become primarily a commercial center. It will become more and more independent, relying less and less on the external market, but you'll always need at least some industry for a well-balanced city.

Commercial zones develop better and faster near the city center. Airports provide a big boost to your city's commerce once your city reaches a population of at least 20,000.

Industry is the manufacture of goods and services to sell. You can sell both to the internal market (within your city) and the external market (outside your city).

Industry is the lifeblood of a small city, and is much more important than commerce while your population is small. When a city is small, there aren't enough customers in it to support itself. You have to manufacture things to sell to the external market and bring in more cash and people. In fact, industry can be thought of as the reason to start a new city.

Industry is a primary source of employment in your city. It is also the primary source of pollution. Industrial areas tend towards low land value and high crime.

The Industry window is an important tool if you want to control the direction of industry in your city. It gives you a readout of the current distribution of industries in your city, as well as the external demand for the products of the various industries. It also lets you set different tax levels for different industries to encourage the ones you want and discourage those you don't. You may want to discourage an industry that causes a lot of pollution. You may want to encourage a small industry that you think may be about to boom.

When you create an industrial zone, the Sims tend to build the industries that are in highest demand. The demand for different industries is related to the era. For example, in 1960, the electronics industry isn't nearly as important, or in as much demand as in 1990.

A forward-thinking mayor in 1930 just may believe that there is a big future in that upstart, tiny electronics industry. Since it is in low demand, the Sims won't invest in it—unless their mayor gives them a tax incentive. So the mayor lowers the tax on the electronics industry and it begins to grow. Thirty years later it begins to bloom, then boom. That's when the mayor raises the taxes and makes a fortune for the city—while securing lots of jobs in a high-tech, still-growing industry.

Another forward-thinking mayor whose city is almost entirely supported by one industry, say automotive, may want to diversify before the market crashes and the city becomes a ghost town.

And yet another forward-thinking mayor may realize that the new high-tech industries won't thrive without an educated population, and will make sure to provide schools, colleges and other educational institutions.

Many aspects of city design affect industry. The presence of hospitals can give a boost to the petrochemical industry (pharmaceuticals). The presence or lack of seaports can help or hinder heavy manufacturing like steel, mining, and automotive. The presence or lack of a good highway and/or rail system can also affect heavy industry's development. City ordinances can also hinder or help various industries.

Power

Yes, cities existed before electricity, but not in SimCity 2000. Sims are electronic life-forms and can't exist without it.

All zones need power to develop—except for military bases. Power lines transfer power between power plants and zones and between non-adjacent zones. Power isn't transferred through adjacent zones or through roads or rails that divide zones without power lines.

Tiles with power lines consume power. If you place too many power lines you waste a lot of power.

The types of power sources available are time-dependent. You can't build a nuclear power plant in 1900. As new technology becomes available, it will be announced in the newspapers. All power plants are introduced when they become cost-efficient— no early, flaky experimental models in this game. Some of SimCity 2000's power sources do not yet exist in the real world. We've made some rough predictions as to when they'll be available and put them into the game. If our predictions are off, sorry—we specialize in simulation, not real stuff. You can mix and match the types of power plants in a single city.

All power plants have a 50-year life span, after which they collapse. When they collapse, they don't cause fires or leak radiation, they just stop working, and you have to rebuild them (and pay for them all over again). You'll receive warnings about aging power plants in the newspapers, and the Query tool will give your plants' exact ages.

If you have the No Disasters setting activated (in the Disasters menu), then plants won't collapse. They'll be automatically rebuilt and you'll be charged. If you don't have the cash to rebuild them, then they'll collapse and you'll be out of power and out of luck. So save up cash for power plant replacement or be ready to issue a bond.

Power is measured in megawatts (Mw). Developed areas require on the average one Mw for three occupied tiles. The exact power consumption varies with time, population density and an occasional city ordinance. Connecting too many buildings to a power source results in brownouts.

Here is a table comparing the different power plants. The years are +/- 10 years.

Type	Year Avail	Mw	Cost	Cost per Mw
Coal	1900	200	$4,000	$20
Hydroelectric	1900	20	$400	$20
Oil	1900	220	$6,600	$30
Gas	1950	50	$2,000	$40
Nuclear	1955	500	$ 15,000	$30
Wind	1980	4	$100	$25
Solar	1990	50	$1,300	$26
Microwave	2020	1600	$ 28,000	$17.5
Fusion	2050	2500	$ 40,000	$16

Coal power is always available, even in 1900, and is fairly efficient, but is the worst polluter.

Hydroelectric power is always available, even in 1900, is fairly efficient, and doesn't pollute. Hydroelectric dams can only be placed on falling water.

Oil power is always available, even in 1900, and pollutes about half as much as coal.

Gas power pollutes even less than oil, but is very inefficient.

Nuclear power is expensive to build and not too efficient, but it puts out a lot of power. There is also the risk of a meltdown disaster. Nuclear power plants are unavailable if you declare your city a nuclear-free zone.

Wind power is fairly efficient and very clean, but puts out very little power, so you'll need a lot of wind generators to produce serious wattage. Wind power is also subject to the whims of the weather. There is more wind at higher altitudes.

Solar power is non-polluting and fairly efficient, but has a low output and is unreliable—very little power is produced when it's cloudy or foggy. A combination of solar and wind power plants can produce a stable energy flow since one generally thrives while the other snoozes.

Microwave power is actually solar power collected by an orbiting satellite and beamed down to a microwave collector disk. It is very efficient and produces a massive amount of power, but is very expensive to "get off the ground," and once in a while the energy beam from the satellite misses the dish. Oops.

Fusion power is very clean and reliable. It is the most efficient power source and produces enough power to run a city half the size of your entire city limits. It is very safe, with no radiation leakage or meltdowns. But it costs a whole heck of a lot of money.

Transportation

People gotta move. Sims gotta move. Products, delivery trucks, construction materials and all kinds of things need to be moved around the city. Transportation is the city's circulation system. Sims won't start developing a zone or building any buildings until there is access to some sort of transportation system.

It not only costs money to build your transportation system, but there is a yearly maintenance fee, found in the Budget window. By examining the Transit Authority books, you can set separate funding levels for roads, highways, rails, subways, bridges and tunnels.

The most basic transportation system consists of roads. Sims won't build buildings that are more than three tiles from a road (or other transportation system), so if you're after density, the largest area that will fully develop is a 6 x 6 square surrounded by road. If you're more interested in aesthetics, then you can make larger squares or rectangles and put parks or forests in the undeveloped center.

Tunnels allow roads to run through mountains instead of going around them. They can be a real convenience, but they can also be expensive. They cost more to build than roads, and their yearly maintenance is higher. Tunnels can't cross each other, even at different altitudes.

When roads carry up to 44 cars per minute, it is considered to be "no traffic." From 44 to 88 cars per minute is light traffic, and above that is heavy traffic. Watch the newspapers for traffic-related stories and check the traffic map in the Map window to find trouble spots. In addition to causing traffic, roads or the cars on them are a major source of pollution in your city.

Once your roads are overloaded, you have a number of options, depending on the year in your city. In 1900 your only transportation options are roads, tunnels, rails and rail depots. Other options become available as new technologies develop. Watch the newspapers for inventions that give you access to new forms of transportation.

These are the years, +/-10 years, when different forms of transportation become available:

1910   Subways and subway stations
1920   Buses and bus depots
1930   Highways and onramps

Buses allow roads to carry more people than roads alone without generating problem traffic. To start a bus line, you need at least one bus depot. Buses leave the depot and let passengers on and off all along the way. There are no animated buses, so the visible effect of a bus depot is a lowering of traffic near the depot. Bus depots must be adjacent to roads. If they are adjacent to onramps or highways but, not a road, they won't be effective. Buses are a more efficient use of gasoline than cars, so they produce much less pollution per passenger. Pollution levels are slightly but noticeably lower around effective bus depots.

Highways are basically two roads, one in each direction, so they are capable of carrying twice as many cars as a road. In addition, because they can travel at a higher speed on a highway, Sims will commute farther on a highway than on a road—up to three times as far. You must provide onramps everywhere you want to let Sims enter or exit the highway. Sims can't travel back and forth between zones and onramps without roads. A highway system is an extension of a road system, not a replacement.

Rails are the paths your trains follow. Sims can only get on or off trains at rail depots. Depots must be adjacent to rails, and you need at least two for a working rail line. Rails can carry many more commuters than roads, plus they are a big boost to heavy industry, allowing shipping of goods and raw materials around the city. Since trains go faster than cars on city streets, Sims will commute farther by train than by car. Compared with cars, trains produce almost no pollution.

Subways are underground rail systems, but are primarily for passengers, and less for the shipping of goods and raw materials. They can be connected directly to rail lines for a continuous flow of train cars. Passengers can only get on and off subways at subway stations. The advantage of subways over other transportation systems is that they are mostly underground. They don't take up valuable real estate. And if you want to add rails to an already developed city, you'll have to tear down a lot of buildings for the rails themselves as well as the large depots. Subways only require small (1 tile) access ways above ground, so they can be added to a city without calling in the wrecking crew. The disadvantage of a subway system is that its very expensive to build and maintain. Subways produce almost no pollution.

When simulating traffic, SimCity 2000 doesn't really simulate every Sim in your city going to work and back and to the store and back and to school and back and to the pub and back and everywhere else they go. With thousands or millions of citizens this would take forever to simulate. The way the traffic model

works is a process called "trip generation" and works on a building-by-building basis. It also works on the assumption that most trips will be from one type of zone to another.

For each building in each zone, the simulator generates trips to both of the other types of zones. If the starting building is a house in a residential zone, the simulation will search out a path to a commercial zone and back, and to an industrial zone and back. It tries to avoid heavy traffic areas, and if it bumps into mass transit there is a 50/50 chance it will take it.

There is a time limit for each trip, and if the time runs out before reaching a zone, then the trip is a failure. The time limit is stable but the allowable distance to the destination depends on the mode of transport. Since highways, rails and subways travel faster than cars on regular roads, the simulation can go up to three times as far while looking for a destination zone.

If a failed trip involves mass transit, then the next time that same building is checked, it won't even try that same type of mass transit.

So the amount of traffic alleviated by mass transit depends on two things:

1. The whims of the Sims—that 50/50 chance.
2. Your city's design—if the bus or train won't get the Sims where they want to go, they'll drive.

A bad mass transit system is worse than none at all, because it won't get used. To promote the use of mass transit as much as possible:

1. Put bus or rail depots or subway stations near busy intersections.
2. Make sure that mass transit lines travel through different types of zones. A bus line that stays in a residential zone won't have much business.

Ports

Airports and seaports are specialized zones. Placing them in areas that are already zoned is a waste of your funds. An airport's primary effect is to boost commerce. Seaports boost industry. Neither type of port is necessary (or affordable) in a very small city.

Once your city starts to grow, your citiSims will let you know when they want ports. The bigger the city, the bigger the ports it will require. Since you can make ports any size you want, and they're very expensive, start small—but leave open space for later expansion. When the city outgrows your small ports, the Sims will let you know when it's time to expand. But if you notice your commercial or industrial zones' growth rate slowing down, you may want to add ports before your Sims ask for them.

Both types of ports produce pollution, but airports pollute more.

Trees

Trees and forests add beauty to your city and its surroundings, and improve property values. They are flammable and can help fires spread.

Water

Lakes, rivers and oceans are sources of drinking water for your city. They also provide recreational areas and tourist attractions, and improve land value.

You can add as much water to your city as you want in Terrain-Editing mode, but once you start a city, it is very expensive, so plan ahead.

Seaports must be on a river or the ocean to be effective, and marinas in the desert are no fun at all.

The Water System

You can build a city without any water system at all, but the population won't grow very dense. A basic water system consists of pumps and pipes. When Sims build buildings, they put in the underground plumbing. All you have to do is add the water mains to connect the buildings to the system and supply the water.

Parts of the water system that are properly supplied with water are animated in light and dark blue. Areas that aren't animated either aren't hooked up or your water source is too small for the population.

Water pumps, when placed away from fresh water act as wells. The amount of water they provide depends on your city's water table and the season. Water pumps placed right next to fresh water (lakes or streams) produce about three times as much as a well on dry land. A pump placed next to salt water (coastline) acts just like a well away from water. To get drinking water from a coastline you need a desalinization plant, which is expensive, but sometimes necessary. Desalinization plants produce twice as much water as a water pump near a river.

Since the amount of water varies with the season, you may end up with shortages during the dry months. Water tanks store water during the wet season so you don't run low in dry times. Another way to prevent droughts is to build a treatment plant to clean and recycle your water.

Recreational Facilities and Open Spaces

Open spaces, whether they are undeveloped greenbelts or manicured recreational facilities, are important to a city, both aesthetically and psychologically. Besides adding land value trees, forests and open space give a city a better feel, an openness that makes citizens feel comfortable and encourages new residents.

As your population rises, your Sims will start demanding recreational facilities. The developed recreation facilities that are available in SimCity 2000 are small parks, big parks, zoos, stadi-

ums and marinas. Recreational facilities are primarily for your city's residents, increasing land value and promoting residential zone growth, but they also influence tourism. Small parks increase land value about the same amount as trees, and big parks increase it twice as much. Marinas, zoos and stadiums are a big boost for residential growth.

The Climate

Even though you don't see the seasons change or the rains fall, and you don't feel the wind blow (other than an occasional tornado or hurricane), there is a climate model in SimCity 2000 that affects your city. Weather reports are available in the newspapers.

Weather trends are generated on a monthly basis, when the simulation looks at the current trend and the season and throws in a certain weighted random element and decides the next trend. The different trends are: cold, clear, hot, foggy, chilly, overcast, snowy, rainy, windy, blizzard, hurricane and tornado. Blizzard, hurricane and tornado are the least likely to occur.

Each trend has a temperature, a wind and a humidity element. In general, temperature affects the water supply, the availability of solar power, and the likelihood of fires and riots; wind affects the availability of wind power, and humidity affects the water supply. These effects combine in various ways in the various trends.

Pollution

Pollution as shown in the maps and graphs is a general overall level combining air, water and noise pollution. The biggest polluters in your city are automobiles, then industry and some types of power plants.

The main things you can do to keep pollution down in your city are to provide good mass transit, opt for low- or non-polluting power sources, and promote low- and non-polluting industries through tax incentives.

Rewards

So you're a great mayor. So you build a great city with the power of your mind and the sweat of your mouse-finger. So your citiSims love you. So what? Where are the perks?

That's where the rewards come in. For the most part the rewards are more for the city than for you personally. Some say that the art and the artist are one, so a reward for your city—your creation— is a reward for you. Others say, "Give me the cash." In any event, there are at least a couple rewards that should give your ego a boost.

Rewards are based on population. As you reach various population levels, you will be notified that a reward is available in a newspaper article and the offering will appear in the submenu under the Rewards button in the City toolbar.

At population:	You get:
2,000	A mayor's house
10,000	City Hall
30,000	Something cool that will boost your ego

When your population reaches 60,000, the military asks you if you want a military base in your city. The pros and cons of military bases are covered later in this manual.

As your city grows, there will be other things that you'll just have to find out for yourself, because I won't tell you. Well, OK. I'll tell you one more: Arcologies at a population of 120,000.

Arcologies are huge, tall, dense cities-in-a-building. They are like a very dense combination residential, commercial and industrial zone. Arcologies are a way to help your population zoom from mere hundreds of thousands to millions, expanding your tax base. There are four different arcologies, designed in 2000, 2050, 2100 and 2150. Even if you have a huge population, you can't build an arcology until it's ready.

Arcologies also spur the growth of nearby residential, commercial and industrial zones. Even though they are theoretically totally contained cities, people who live inside will come out to shop and see the sights, and may even work outside. Others may live outside and work inside.

They look cool too. Unfortunately, arcologies have all the problems of an extremely dense city: lots of crime, pollution and traffic. Technically, arcologies have their own internal police force and traffic system, but there is always an overspill of criminals, travelers and fun-seekers. Make sure you have police coverage near arcologies and that there is ample public transportation surrounding them.

Military Bases

When your population reaches 60,000, the government will ask if you will grant land for a military base. Depending on the base and your plans for your city, this can be a good thing or a bad thing.

When you grant land to the military, you don't choose what type of base you get or where it goes—the government does. The types of bases are: army, navy, air force, and missile silos. If your city is on the coast, the odds are that you will get a naval base. If you don't get a naval base, then if your city is fairly flat, you'll most likely get an air force base, and if it is fairly hilly, you'll get an army base. If it's very hilly, you'll probably get missile silos.

The good parts about a military base are that it gives a boost to your local commerce both by bringing in extra customers for the stores and services in your city, and by supplying civilian jobs. The presence of a military base (other than missile silos) also has a deterrent effect on the monster, and may encourage it to leave sooner. During an emergency, you may also be able to deploy military troops to aid your fire and police departments with the Emergency button.

The bad parts of a military base are a possible increase in crime (wild times on shore leave and civilian crooks preying on soldiers) and traffic congestion.

Missile silos are the least desirable base, since they don't have a big enough staff to have an effect on your economy and they're useless against monsters—these missiles would do more damage to your city than to the monster. Even if your city is a nuclear-free zone, you risk getting missile silos if you agree to a military base.

Education

Education in SimCity 2000 is expressed as an Educational Quotient, or EQ. The higher the EQ, the more educated your population is. You can see a readout of your citiSims' EQ in the population window. EQs range from zero (brain dead) to 150. The equivalent of a high school education is an EQ of 90. A four-year college degree is an EQ of about 140. The SimNational average EQ is 100.

A high EQ is a source of pride to your citizens. It makes your city a more attractive place to raise their children. It also attracts high-tech industry. A low EQ is a source of embarrassment and causes insulting stories to appear in your local (and unread) newspaper. A city with a low EQ has a higher likelihood of both unemployment and rioting.

When you start a new city, the Sims who move in and start their new lives are at least somewhat educated, so you don't have to build schools right away. But don't wait too long, or your settlers' children will be ignorant.

If you have no schools or colleges, then education consists solely of verbal lore passed down from generation to generation, and children will only achieve about 20% of their parents' EQ.

Schools each service a population up to about 15,000, depending on the age distribution of your citizens. Enough schools with full funding can increase your city's EQ up to 90 over a period of years.

Colleges each service a population of up to 50,000, and can eventually increase your city's EQ to as much as 140, but only if you have enough well-funded schools to prepare students for college.

After Sims graduate high school or college, their EQ will slowly erode. The presence of libraries and museums stops this erosion.

All educational facilities raise the local land value, and require yearly funding in the Budget window to remain effective.

City Services

City services consist of police and fire protection, hospitals and prisons. All city services require yearly funding in the Budget window to be fully effective. The locations and effective areas of city services can be seen in the Map window.

Police stations lower the crime rate and raise the land value in a radius around each station. They have the most effect right near the station, and less as distance from the station increases. The locations of police stations, their coverage and the crime rate can be seen in the Map window by using the submenu under the Crime button.

Each police station has a small jail where prisoners are kept. As a city grows and if crime runs rampant, the small jails will be so full and the police will be spending so much time taking care of the prisoners that their efficiency and area of coverage will go down. At this point you can either build a lot more police stations or build a prison. In SimCity 2000, prisons raise the efficiency and effectiveness of your police departments—but only if there is a lot of crime. Prisons are no help to cities with low crime or small populations. If and when your prison gets too full, the newspaper will let you know.

The presence of fire stations makes fires go out sooner, helps prevent fires from occurring in the first place, and raises land value. They have the most effect near the station. The locations of

fire stations and their coverage can be seen in the Map window by using the submenu under the City Services button.

Hospitals keep your Sims healthy, fix them when they're broken, and raise their Life Expectancy (LE). A fully funded hospital can serve a population of 25,000 Sims. You can see the effect of hospitals on your population's LE in the population window. If you don't have a hospital, your city's LE will slowly decline to about 35. If you have enough fully funded hospitals the LE will slowly climb to 85. There are also city ordinances (in the Ordinance window) that can have a positive effect on your city's LE.

Newspapers

Your city's newspapers are your link to your citizens. Reading them keeps you informed, not only of current events, new inventions, city-development announcements and other important or disastrous occurrences, but also of public-opinion polls. Watch your papers closely to see what is important to your Sims.

The newspapers change every month, so reading them all can be time consuming—but useful. If you activate Subscription in the Newspaper menu, your paper will be delivered twice a year. If you activate Extra!!! in the Newspaper menu, then papers announcing important events—inventions and rewards for city growth—will appear. Otherwise, you will have to open the Newspaper menu and select the paper you want to read. Newspapers announcing disasters will always appear.

The different papers (once your city is big enough to have more than one) will have different angles on stories, so you may want to read through more than one.

Inventions

As time passes, things are invented. These inventions give you access to new technologies that you can incorporate into your city. As the technologies become available, new tools will appear in the submenus under the buttons in the City toolbar. Inventions are announced in newspaper Extra!!! editions.

Here are the inventions and their approximate discovery dates,
+/-10 years.

Subway systems	1910
Buses and bus depots	1920
Highways	1930
Water treatment plants	1935
Gas power plants	1950
Nuclear power plants	1955
Wind power plants	1980
Solar power plants	1990
Desalinization plants	1990
Arcologies	2000, 2050, 2100, 2150
Microwave power plants	2020
Fusion power plants	2050

Speed Issues

SimCity 2000 is a very complex simulation. It is also in 256 colors. Both these facts require a lot of computer power. The actual time it takes for a year to pass in your city depends on a number of things, including:

- The type of microprocessor in your computer. SimCity 2000 runs on a wide variety of computers. The more powerful your microprocessor, the faster time will pass.

- The microprocessor's clock speed. The faster the processor, the faster the simulation will run.

- The resolution of your screen and the size of your monitor. Depending on your computer, you may be running SimCity 2000 in as low as 512 x 384 pixel resolution or as high as 1280 x 1024 or more. The higher the resolution, the more dots SimCity 2000 has to draw on your screen, and the slower it will go. Of course the speed of your computer and your graphics card may make up for lost time.

- The size of your city. The simulation model spends a lot more time and does a lot more calculations on tiles that are developed than on bare land tiles. In a busy city that fills the

whole city limits, time will pass much, much slower than in a tiny town. Ways to make the simulation go faster include:

- Setting the speed to Cheetah in the Speed menu.
- Keeping the City window small.
- Keeping as few windows as possible open at a time.
- Turning off both Subscription and Extra!!! in the Newspaper menu.
- Turning off Music and Sound Effects (in the Options menu) helps a little.

But then again, sometimes you don't want time to pass too fast, especially when disasters are sweeping through your city or when you are trying to keep your city center from decaying. In these times of need, you can always open the Speed menu and slow things down—or even stop them entirely.

A major factor in urban planning is the NIMBY factor: not in my back yard. The courts are full of cases where developers had the blessings of local planning boards, met county zoning regulations and promised to inject new life and money into a community—but the citizens didn't want whatever it was in their neighborhood. This goes for luxury hotels as well as prisons, nuclear power plants and toxic waste dumps. XX

The first thing to do is decide what kind of city you want to build. Once you know what your long-term goals are, you can best plan your strategy.

If you want to grow your population as large as possible, then zone densely, keep control of crime, and watch the newspapers for public opinion and important inventions. If you want to make a lot of money, then tax your subjects until they scream and keep your spending to a minimum. If you want to create a city that you'd like to live in, then keep your eye on the newspapers for public opinion, and mentally put yourself in your Sims' places.

Once you start to build, stay small and go easy on the infrastructure. Keep your costs down. You want to get out of the red and into the black as soon as possible. Show a little patience and build up a good reserve of funds.

As you build, try not to make large, densely concentrated areas. The denser the population of an area, the more pollution and the more crime you have. Try to find a happy medium between suburban sprawl and super-dense city.

Remember that not only does it cost to build city infrastructure, but it costs to maintain it.

If you need to skimp on city services, go ahead, but keep your police well-funded. If your town is small or you have a lot of police stations, you may not need to keep them fully-funded, but be careful. Use the Query tool in the City toolbar to see your police stations' effectiveness. If the arrests are equal to the crimes, you can try lowering the funding for a while. Once the arrests fall behind the crimes, add more funding or more police stations. High crime destroys land value, chasing out some of your population and lowering your tax income.

Skimping on fire department funding is a little less drastic, but can be dangerous. Do so at your Sims' risk. You can turn off disasters in the Disasters menu—if you're a wimp.

Try to maintain high land values to keep those property taxes coming in. But be sure to zone for some low-cost housing, since all your Sims can't afford to buy luxury homes on waterfront property.

Remember that you have to replace your power plants every 50 years. Buying the big expensive power plants is more efficient as far as cost per megawatt, but only if your city is large enough to need all that power.

You need a good balance of the three basic zones, with the number of tiles zoned residential approximately equal to the total tiles zoned commercial and industrial. In a small city, you'll need more industrial than commercial. You'll need equal numbers of each at a population of about 100,000. Above that, lean more towards commercial. The Demand Indicator in the City toolbar lets you know which zones you should be adding.

Try to work with the land instead of using brute force to overpower it. You'll not only end up with a much more "organic" looking and feeling city, but it'll save you a lot of money. Best yet, pick—or build—a beautiful site for your city before you start to build.

As for the actual layout of your city, maps of cities from all over the world are easily available. Start with your favorite city and improve on it.

Try the modular approach. First try to design a small, compact "neighborhood," complete with all the zones, transportation and city services you need, that runs very efficiently, or better yet, at a profit. Then copy the pattern of that neighborhood all over the place. Place them strategically so they can share the high-cost city items like schools, colleges, museums and power plants.

Above all, use your imagination.

Unless you have No Disasters set in the Disasters menu, disasters just happen. The disasters that are connected with a scenario happen even when you have disasters turned off. So there. If you're the adventurous type (or just plain mean) you can set off your own disasters from the Disasters menu and test your preparedness, your quick thinking and the robustness of your city's design. Not all disasters are available in the Disasters menu.

Certain conditions in your city attract or discourage disasters, and certain city events can even cause them. So, to a certain extent, you can prepare for and even lessen the likelihood of disasters.

In the event of a disaster, the first thing to do is stop any fires that you can. Next, rebuild the utilities, then the transportation system. Be ready to jump on that Emergency button in the City toolbar. It will let you deploy your fire, police and sometimes the military to areas of need, but be careful where you put them. In general, firemen are good at fighting fires, but can be wiped out by rioters; police are good at controlling riots, but can get burnt up in a fire. Both fire and police can handle the manual labor of building dams to help fight floods. If you have a military base, you may have access to troops during an emergency. Military troops are capable of anything police or firemen can do, just not quite as specialized or effective.

Where a disaster causes destruction in a zone, you must manually bulldoze the rubble in Demolish/Clear mode before the zone will begin to rebuild.

FIRES

Fires are most likely to occur when the weather is hot and you don't have good fire department coverage. Fires are also the byproducts of other disasters including air crashes, riots and tornadoes. You can fight fires by using the Emergency button in the City toolbar and blocking their path with the Emergency Fire

icons. As tiles burn up, move in and surround the fires. Dispatching your police to the scene of the fire can help keep cars and crowds away and let the firemen do their jobs, but police can't fight fire. If you have the right kind of military base, the Emergency button may give you access to military troops to help fight fires.

FLOODS

Floods occur in the wet season, and can be the byproducts of hurricanes, tidal waves or tornadoes. They are most likely to occur on the coastline, but occasionally a river will flood. There's not much you can do once a flood begins, but you can prepare for the worst. Floods only destroy things at sea level. Your buildings that are even one tile up will weather the storm. Since seaports must be at sea level, they are prime targets for flood damage. If you have a river, try building your seaports upriver, away from the coast. You can also use the Raise Terrain mode of the Bulldozer tool to build protective dikes in areas that you think might flood. You can try deploying your police and fire departments with the Emergency tool to help build dams to hold back floods. You might lose a few civil servants, but it should slow the advance of the flood.

RIOTS

The main causes of riots are heat, high crime and unemployment. Riots can also occur if your city has a long blackout. A good economy and a low crime rate are the best ways to prevent riots. And keep your power going. You can fight riots with the Emergency button and your police departments the same way you'd fight a fire with your fire departments. Fires are byproducts of riots.

AIR CRASHES

Sometimes planes or helicopters crash. Other than a smashed building here and there, the main danger from an air crash is fire. Put out the fire as quickly as you can, then hold an investigation and call it pilot error. If a plane crashed at the airport, fire the air traffic controller.

TORNADOES AND HURRICANES

Tornadoes and hurricanes occur because of climatic conditions, and cannot be prevented. Keep an eye on the weather reports of high winds in the newspaper and you might receive enough warning to reinforce your police and fire departments in time. While they are very different in the real world, as far as their effect in SimCity 2000 goes, they are pretty much the same, except that tornadoes cause a narrow path of destruction and hurricanes can really mess up the place.

EARTHQUAKES

Once again, there's nothing you can do to prevent them. All you can do is treat the symptoms—and those are many. Earthquakes not only shake down buildings and damage your city's infrastructure (roads, rails, power lines, etc.), but cause fires, looting and riots. All you gotta do is put out the fires, restore power and transport, control the mobs and rebuild your city.

NUCLEAR MELTDOWN

If you have a nuclear power plant, there is a slight chance that it will melt down. If it does, your city is in real trouble. There will be a big explosion, fires will break out, and radiation will spread and contaminate the surrounding land and water. The radiation lasts many generations. Neither you nor your Sims can build on contaminated ground.

Don't confuse the end of your power plants' workable life span with a disaster. Even though your nuclear plants will stop working and blow up after 50 years, there is no danger, other than from blackouts or brownouts. This is just the plant wearing out, not blowing up, melting down or leaking.

Fusion plants don't melt down and don't leak radiation, only fission (standard nuclear) plants.

OOPS

The microwave power plant has its accidents, too. On occasion the beam of energy from the satellite misses the collector dish and causes some inconvenient death and destruction. There's nothing you can do to prevent it, but put the fires out as soon as you can. Play it safe and build microwave power plants out in the boonies.

THE MONSTER

The monster is an intelligent creature from outer space. But then again, it might just be a Hollywood movie special effect run amok. Since we seem incapable of communicating with it, we don't know if it is really out to destroy our cities or if it just doesn't understand that we find it unpleasant to be smashed, set on fire or whisked away to another planet. The presence of certain military bases may deter the monster or rush it on its way. Maybe if you could make it understand that its behavior is antisocial, it will stop. But then again, maybe not.

OTHERS

There are a number of other disasters that will pop up from time to time in SimCity 2000, but you'll find out all about them in your own good time.

GALLERY

As always, we wanted to put something extra into this manual; something to enhance the "city" experience of SimCity 2000.

In the past we have included history or background sections, researched and written by one person—but this time we're taking our cue from the city itself.

All the great cities of the world—Athens, London, Amsterdam, New York, Vienna, Paris, and the others— were not designed by one person. They are the products of many people over a long period of time.

In this light, our "added value" section has become a gallery of pictures, poems, quotes, and essays, by a number of people. All the exhibits in this gallery have one thing in common: they deal in some way with people's experiences of and feelings about cities.

Much of the Gallery is located on the following pages, but there are other pictures, writings and quotes sprinkled all throughout the earlier parts of this manual.

UNTITLED

Carry me over the planate tops
Of steel, brick and elemental rock
Peppered lights dazzle the Moorish sky
As I gaze through the magnified eyes of flight
My city looks up, with Byzantine eyes
Lapping the world as I ascend its sky

Sweet ladies stroll through
        the bright nights of Astor
Children of St. Mark's rollick there
Where strangers flock for a roll in the city
Through the breeze of its rhythm they dare
Silky fingers count a midnight take
Jackal eyes attend a back-street wake

Some mock my city as cloying, calling it elite
But this salient hub does not weep, nor sleep
        nor die at night
It dreams—alive, with lusty insomniac satyrs
Adroitly dancing in the
        cool lower eastside breeze
On the auspicious wings of flight, belted
        down
Above the womb of eight million children

Self-Portrait in the City — Barbara Pollak, Pencil on Cardstock

My sad yet ecstatic eyes linger, nostalgic
As I whirl East to the land of the rising sun
To study the art of thin needles
        and pressing thumbs
I hang my claws—adorn sentient eyes
And to the beast below
My wicked city—good-by

           — David Caggiano

*David's poem recounts his mixed emo-
tions as he prepares to move from loose
and wild New York City to a disciplined
way of life in Mishima Japan (to study
shiatsu and acupuncture). Barbara draws
a hopeful picture of her San Francisco
home while on the facing page Larry
expresses a far dimmer view.*

The Blind Man Stops to Listen — Larry Wilson, Graphite and Chinese White

BIG CITY BLUES
by Tom Bentley

I had never considered myself that much of a tenderfoot. I thought that the transition from years of Santa Cruzing to the streets of San Francisco would be no great shakes. Heckfire, I'd grown up in the suburbs of big-city Long Beach—I knew the subtle bitternesses of a neighbor's more perfectly trimmed lawn—and San Francisco couldn't be much more daunting. Well, I had barely straightened the books on my San Francisco shelves before some of the local educators began tutoring me in the curious scholarship of the streets.

My first lesson was about school hours—all instruction occurs between two and six in the morning. I discovered that I had been leading the dullest of lives in Santa Cruz. Here I was, *sleeping,* when I could have joined the teams of people who thump their fists on the trunklids of cars, yodel, or release the primal scream they had saved up just for my neighborhood. One recent bottomless night some woman stood on the opposite street corner, plaintively crying out the name of her daughter (or her schnauzer, or her goldfish, who knows) for twenty-five minutes, without relent.

Another wee-hour walker strode up and down my block shouting "I'm gonna kick your butt," for half an hour; the owner of the threatened rear never materialized. Deep into another evening some passionate fellow rambled up and down the block announcing—with the subtle vocalizations of a drunken football fan—that he wanted some very specific oral attention. I can't verify the success of his quest.

Now these are simply highlights of what is an almost nightly schedule of activity; often it is just animated conversation (at death-of-etiquette volume), ghetto-blaster thunder, or unintelligible gruntings. Occasionally, some true urban ugliness crops up, such as when I had to ask some gentle-man who was throttling his date below my second-story window to please seek some other means of expressing his affection. The scary moments are when you hear tremendous cursing and scuffling and then absolute silence—did the streets claim another soul? These things spur some questions: Am I missing out on some jolly fun? When do these people sleep? How do they pay for all that cocaine? What threat did the citizens of Spain use to get the mayor to agree to allow practice for the running of the bulls at Pamplona through my neighborhood at three a.m.?

Just as interesting as the curbside caterwauling before dawn's dress is what you might find on the sidewalk the next morning. Huge console TVs with the picture tube stove in. Three-legged chairs. Headless dolls. It's a bit like a down-at-heel flea market, only there's no merchant around to take any offers. Then the next morning it will all be gone, like a one-night movie set.

One morning I gaped for ten minutes in complete bewilderment at what looked like an enormous street salad on the corner. Broad swaths of mayonnaise and salsa seven or eight feet long, like a Jackson Pollock painting. Huge clumps of broccoli scattered many feet apart. Big chunks of salmon pitched about at random. It looked like a shopper had been scooped up at tremendous velocity by a UFO, but that the groceries were discarded as they swooped away. Time it was that I would become incensed when beer-brained dolts on their way to the beach would toss their bottles onto my lawn in Santa Cruz—here, people leave a lifetime's worth of clothing in the center of the sidewalk, a sidewalk as likely as not to be sprinkled with the shattered remains of bottles tossed blithely to their deaths.

Of course, you don't get to see the glass on the sidewalk when the cars are parked on *top* of it. Now, in sweet old Santa Cruz I would screech when I would return from some summertime errand and ave to park *across the street* because some beach-bound yahoos had snagged all the spots in front of my house. Well, I have been educated to understand that a parking spot across the street from my house is sweeter than music from Apollo's lute—I feel almost guilty not having to drive around the block, and then the next block, and then .... Your entire *world* here is dependent upon your parking situation. Heard of a good restaurant four miles away? Walk, my friend. Going to a job interview at ten? Better leave at seven-thirty, just in case the parking is bad. Want to eat in Chinatown on a weekend? Stay at home and cook Top Ramen. In my neighborhood people park around corners, in crosswalks, in front of hydrants, on the sidewalk—you could make some serious money if you could invent a cheap, lightweight, ramped platform to park above other cars.

That is, as long as someone wasn't sleeping upon the bottom car. I had always considered the street-people situation in Santa Cruz to be a difficult and sad circumstance with no easy solution. Well, the street people in Santa Cruz seem like silk-bedecked barons in comparison to the street people in San Francisco. These are not people marching to a different drummer; they are waltzing to an occult orchestra. Here are folks with lightning storms in their heads, shouting their pain in tangled syntax no linguist could untwist. Some very bad cases look almost like sacks of rust and mold. Human detritus—pained, purposeless, and defined by the lack of something I take for granted, a home.

Yet, if it is an unusual look you seek, the street people take a back seat to some of the deliberate productions of antic appearance seen in this fair city. Sure, Santa Cruz has its share of outlandishly or eccentrically or even frighteningly haired hipsters, but they are Lady Di's in waiting next to some of the rare specimens here. Here we have people who look as though a wombat with delerium tremens razored across their heads. Here are hair-cuts that cost one hundred dollars but had to have been rendered with plumber's tools and glue. Upon these heads rest colors never known to nature. Here are people who dye their nostril hair orange. I love them.

And for any of you Santa Cruz types who were worried that your wardrobe of black jackets, shirts, pants, and boots was on its way out, don't fret—one look around the Haight and you can confidently see that the sweetly cadaverous look, a kind of Lazarus in black leather, has never been more richly represented. Dye your tongues black and come here; no one would blink an eye.

You know, it seems like I'm complaining about the education I'm getting. Nah, it's been worth every sleepless night. Almost. And, jeepers, when I top a hill on my bicycle and catch a glimpse of the sun slapping the riffled waters of the bay and the shoulders of the great Golden Gate thrown back, I get a strong sense of place and rightness. It sounds completely corny, but there's a certain sustenance and a kind of odd, quiet glory here. It's enough to go on with things, at least until the next band of recreational honkers (I'm convinced there's a sign on the freeway directing them to my block) drives up and down making merry on their horns.

But I do miss the loveliness and charm of Santa Cruz. I marvel when I think of the things I use to complain about there. It's a different world, but so easy to visit. Save me a parking place.

This essay, first published in Good Times, a Santa Cruz, CA newspaper, is one man's musings on moving from the small town of Santa Cruz to big, bustling San Francisco. Mr. Bentley recently returned from a night out on the town in San Francisco, and having driven for eleven hours straight in search of a parking place, he drove back to Santa Cruz and has once again taken up residence there. No guts, no glory.

CHOKING

Choking on the
N.Y. skyline,
taxis leering
wide-mouthed
down the boulevard,
you hold my hand,
memories piled
in barricades—
brittle, quick,
cutting and loving.

On the acrid
pavement,
we breathe
the shallow air,
dry bones
and memories
collapsing,
arming.
Taxis tear echoes
from the buildings—
words
fail.

— Margo Lockwood
August 1992

Cityscape 1 — Emily Friedman, Photograph

N.Y. DAWN

5 am
in your loft,
water banging
down
fire
escapes
empty,
as this
room.

the hissing rain
whispers
dionysian
drum solos.
new york city
gnashes her teeth,
buried
alive
under blue
water
running...

it is
almost like silence,
a thousand
conversations
on rooftops
and windows.
almost like silence,
this roar
of solitude.

— Margo Lockwood
        to Lisa Lee
        January 16, 1985

Cityscape 2 — Emily Friedman, Photograph

CITIES OF TOMORROW
by Keith Ferrell

Do cities even *have* futures? Of course they do: it's just that the future isn't what it used to be.

And what exactly did our metropolitan future 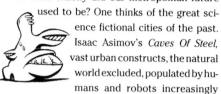 used to be? One thinks of the great science fictional cities of the past. Isaac Asimov's *Caves Of Steel*, vast urban constructs, the natural world excluded, populated by humans and robots increasingly hard to tell apart.

Or Robert Silverberg's urban monads from his *World Inside* series: huge arcologies climbing hundreds of stories toward the sky, self-contained worlds in themselves.

H.G. Wells, who knew more about the future than most of us, made his urban vision tacit in his only original film: *The Shape Of Things To Come.* Watch the final segment of the film as the camera pursues a long, prowling pan through a fabulous science fiction city, the more fabulous for the fact that in the movie's context it has been built upon the ashes of global conflagration.

Or the many World's Fair portrayals over the years, each more elaborate than those previous, showing pristine cities overflown by airborne taxis, skyscrapers become delicate spires flung skyward, architecturally celebrating both the human and the urban experience.

Now visit a real city.

How different the reality is: smelly, dirty, dangerous, crumbling, abandoned by business, fled by families who can afford to flee.

Who would live in such a place?

Youth, that's who.

The artistic and ambitious young have always been attracted to cities, undeterred by danger—perhaps, indeed, drawn by it. There is a pulse and a power to all but the most defeated of urban areas,

a sense of risk and excitement, adventure and opportunity.

And it draws the young like magnets.

Visit any of the world's great cities: Tokyo, London, Los Angeles, Rio, San Francisco, Paris, Cairo, Moscow, Hong Kong, or New York—*always,* always and above all New York, the Apple, the one true capital of the planet—and take a walk. Don't restrict yourself to the tourist paths.

Keep your eyes open. Look at the boutiques and shops (*not* just the chain outlets) catering to the young, often owned by the young themselves. Stroll through a gallery and marvel at the freshness and impudence of the new generation of artists.

Keep your ears open. Listen to the music coming from small clubs or basement apartments, kids wrestling with craft as well as art. Drop into a bookstore and eavesdrop on a pretentious but sincere conversation or two. Grab one of the free newspapers that seem to bloom in every city in the world, read it with your ears as well as your eyes. Listen to what they're saying: find out what's important to the kids, why they've come to the city, what they hope to accomplish.

Keep your heart open. Walk through a park late on a spring afternoon. Bask in the radiance given off by young lovers, in the city seeking the realization of shared dreams.

Cities call out to youth. That's been true since cities first existed, and it will remain true as long as cities exist. If you want to discover the next generation of *anything,* go to a city.

But what about the other side? The dark side of our cities? The danger? The dirt? The deprivation? The despair?

In other words, the challenges we face, we who love cities and live in them, and also those who've fled them but still must deal with the consequences that flow from urban areas.

Again, look to youth. It is worse than a cliché to state that the young are our greatest resource, but the thing about clichés is that they generally contain a core of truth. Well, for our future cities, we need to consider those artistic and ambitious youths to be an urban core—or corps!—of truth. We need to enlist their energies in combat against that dirt and despair, in opposition to the deprivation and the danger.

Youth knows no better, you know? Youth doesn't know that these problems are insoluble, are only going to get worse. Youth—the best of youth—believes that problems are meant to be solved, and understands that solutions must be *sought*, not legislated. They have energy, they have enthusiasm, they have ideas—in short they possess everything that's needed to approach the dilemmas of urban life and, maybe, make a difference.

Cities also entrap youth. There are young people in our cities who aren't artistically enfranchised, who aren't ambitious in any acceptable sense. Who have not *come* to the city, but are *trapped* there. Not even or not really *youth:* the word does not apply because they have been afforded no opportunity to *be* youthful. Who've been beaten from birth and who in what is all too often a single blinding instant of violence find themselves without option other than to beat back. Their souls—their potential and promise, their chance of creating art, participating in commerce, and discovering their gifts—are lost without ever having had the chance to grow.

Too often—indeed, almost constantly—it's that blinding flash of violence that becomes, via the media, *the* image of our cities. Yet cities have *always* been violent; the violence is part of the package that comes with assembling a large population in a central area.

That violent image, though, is why, as youth moves into late youth and early middle age, as artistic ambition becomes career, young love burgeons into family, as in other words life goes on, too, much of that vibrant life leaves the cities. Leaves just as artistic and intellectual peaks and primes are being attained. Leaves for the suburbs which offer the succor of comfortability, but lack the pulse, the drive, the excitement of the city. They depart the domain of dreams.

And therein lies, at this moment in history, the urban rub. The people most able to do something about urban problems are those most likely—and most able—to leave urban areas.

What's needed—and I believe that we are beginning to see hints of this becoming an actuality—is gathering collaboration between and among the energies and enthusiasms of the most capable of our urban young, and the potentials and problems of the disenfranchised. We must pursue a matchmaking of the capable with those who do not yet know that they, too, are capable—and capable of creating wonders.

Unrealistic? No doubt—but what could be more unrealistic in the first place than the creation of cities? Who could possibly expect conglomerations of millions, or *tens* of millions of that most contentious of creatures, the human being, to work at all, much less work well.

Yet they do work, and they can work well. Cities both call to youth and entrap youth. The challenge that we face is one of ensuring that those who most clearly hear the cities' call are not lost just as they become best able to approach the cities' problems, to free those who are trapped there. Then, and only then, will we begin to get a glimpse—there, on the horizon, to be strived for if never fully obtained—of the cities of our dreams, the real cities of tomorrow.

Keith Ferrell is the Editor of OMNI Magazine, author of more than a dozen books, and a leading young futurist who loves cities very much indeed. The cartoons by John "Bean" Hastings are part of a set, which are spread throughout the manual.

William Holiday, Crayon on Paper

These drawings show just how differently two people can view the same city.

7-year-old William Holliday describes his picture as "the bad part of town," with people begging for money, getting drugs, smoking and drinking. The sun is trying to get through the polluted sky. In the background the buildings are run down, deserted—nobody wants to live there. The cars look like bumper cars because of all the wrecks they've been in.

10-year-old Joey Holliday's drawing shows an entusiastic view of New York City, complete with the Empire State Building, the Statue of Liberty, and the Twin Towers.

Joey Holiday, Crayon on Paper

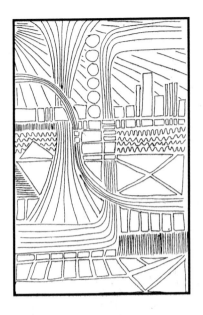

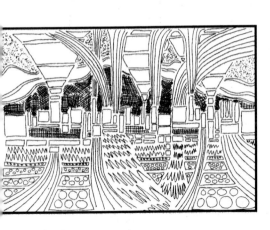

Cityscapes — James Hewes, Etchings

SIM CITY 2000

Appendix

From SimCity to SimCity 2000

If you're already familiar with SimCity or SimCity Classic, then take a quick look through this Appendix. It lists some of the most important changes and additions to SimCity 2000. If they were all listed here it'd take away the fun of discovery—and repeat 3/4 of the manual.

New Help System
Just hold down either Shift key and click on any button or tool for an on-screen explanation of what it does and how it works.

THE EDIT WINDOW HAS BEEN REPLACED BY THE CITY WINDOW
Edit window replaced by City window, which has a new isometric perspective, three levels of magnification, and the ability to rotate the land. Unlike the Edit window, the City window is always open and always active, even when other windows cover parts of it.

ENHANCED TOOLBAR
The Toolbar in the City window has added features, and many more variations with pop-up submenus under many of the buttons.

TERRAIN EDITOR
All the terrain-editing tools you could ever want are built right in. No separate Terrain Editor program is necessary.

ZONING
Now, instead of plopping down zones in preset sizes, you draw the rectangle on the map to set your zones to any size and almost any shape you want. And each of the three basic zones (residential, commercial and industrial) can be zoned either light or dense. You can run roads and power lines right through zones and you can zone right over roads, power lines, hills, valleys and forests. Power no longer travels from empty zone to empty zone without power lines, but it will travel from building to building to adjacent zones.

THE LAND HAS ALTITUDE
The land now has 32 levels of altitude, so you can build your city on mountains or plains.

AN UNDERGROUND LEVEL
There is an underground layer for the water system (yes, that's new, too) and subways (so are they).

TRAINS, SUBWAYS, DEPOTS AND STATIONS
Trains have been joined by subways for mass transit systems, but don't expect them to start running when you set down tracks—you need stations and depots for passengers to get on and off.

POP-UP AND TEAR-OFF WINDOWS
Some of the toolbar buttons pop up small windows that remain on the screen only as long as you are holding the mouse button. Windows can also be opened so they stay open until you close them—in two ways. Either click and drag their button in the toolbar, or select them in the Windows menu.

THE NEWSPAPERS HAVE REPLACED THE EVALUATION WINDOW
Keep an eye on the newspapers for public opinion as well as other important news that will affect your city.

NEW CITY SERVICES
In addition to police and fire stations, you are responsible for both hospitals and prisons.

NEW EDUCATION SYSTEM AND RECREATIONAL FACILITIES
You can place schools, colleges, libraries and museums to build your city's educational system. And your entertainment options include parks, zoos, stadiums and marinas.

NEW POPULATION WINDOW
You can survey your population for their age ranges, their life expectancy and their level of education.

NEW INDUSTRY WINDOW

You can survey the different types of industries in your city, see the national demand for different industrial products, and manipulate the tax rates to encourage or discourage different industries.

NEW NEIGHBORS WINDOW

Your city is no longer alone. You can see your surrounding cities and their populations.

NEW ORDINANCE WINDOW

Now you can push different ordinances through your city council that will either bring more money into your city (like a sales tax) or improve the quality of life of your citiSims (like pro-reading campaigns and neighborhood watch programs).

NEW FINANCE FEATURES

The Budget window has been greatly enhanced, with more items and more control.

GO PLAY ALREADY!

Enough of this skulking around in the Appendix—go play the game!

Bibliography

Alexander, Christopher. *A New Theory of Urban Design.* Oxford University Press, 1987.

Alexander, Christopher, et al. *A Pattern Language.* Oxford University Press, 1977.

Ausubel, Jesse H., and Herman, Robert, Editors. *Cities and their Vital Systems, Infrastructure Past, Present, and Future.* Washington, D.C.: National Academy Press, 1988.

Banfield, Edward C. *The Unheavenly City.* Boston: Little, Brown and Company, 1968.

Boyer, R., and D. Savageau. *Places Rated Almanac.* Chicago: Rand McNally & Co., 1986.

Callenbach, Ernest. *Ecotopia.* Berkeley: Banyan Tree Books,1975.

Choay, Francoise. *The Modern City: Planning in the 19th Century.* New York: George Braziller, 1969.

Clapp, James A. *The City, A Dictionary of Quotable Thoughts on Cities and Urban Life.* Center for Urban Policy Research, Rutgers University, New Brunswick, 1984.

Clark, David. *Urban Geography.* Baltimore: The Johns Hopkins University Press, 1982.

Clay, Grady. *Close-Up, How to Read the American City.* Chicago: The University of Chicago Press, 1980.

Gallion, A., and S. Eisner. *The Urban Pattern.* New York: Van Nostrand Reinhold Company, 1986.

Greenburg, M., D. Krueckeberg, and C. Michaelson. *Local Population and Employment Projection Techniques.* New Brunswick: Center for Urban Policy Research, 1987.

Hoskin, Frank P. *The Language of Cities.* Cambridge: Schenkman Publishing Company, Inc., 1972.

Jacobs, Jane. *The Death and Life of Great American Cities.* New York: Vintage Books, 1961.

Jacobs, Jane. *The Economy of Cities.* New York: Vintage Books, 1970.

Krueckeberg, Donald. *Urban Planning Analysis: Methods and Models.* New York: John Wiley & Sons, 1974.

Le Corbusier. *The City of Tomorrow and Its Planning.* New York: Dover Publications, Inc., 1987.

Register, Richard. *Ecocity Berkeley.* Berkeley: North Atlantic Books, 1987.

Rudofsky, Bernard. *Architecture Without Architects.* New York: Doubleday & Company, 1964.

Spreiregen, Paul D., AIA. *Urban Design: The Architecture of Towns and Cities,* New York: McGraw-Hill, 1965.

Warner, Sam Bass, Jr., Editor. *Planning for a Nation of Cities,* Cambridge, MA: The M.I.T. Press, 1966.

Whittick, Arnold, Editor-In-Chief. *Encyclopedia of Urban Planning.* New York: McGraw-Hill, 1974.

Planning (The magazine of the American Planning Association), 1313 E. 60th St. Chicago, IL 60637

RELATED READING FOR CHILDREN, FICTION AND NON-FICTION

Barker, Albert. *From Settlement to City.* New York: Julian Messner, 1978.

Burton, Virginia Lee. *The Little House.* Boston: Houghton Mifflin, 1942 (reissued 1969).

Dr. Seuss. *The Lorax.* New York: Random House, 1971.

Eichner, James A. *The First Book of Local Government.* New York: Franklin Watts, 1976.

Macaulay, David. *City: A Story of Roman Planning and Construction.* Boston: Houghton Mifflin, 1974.

Macaulay, David. *Underground.* Boston: Houghton Mifflin, 1976.

Monroe, Roxie. *Architects Make Zigzags: Looking at Architecture from A to Z.* Washington D.C.: National Trust for Historic Preservation, 1986.

Murphy, Shirley, and P. Murphy. *Mrs. Tortino's Return to the Sun.* Shepard Books, 1980.

Rhodes, Dorothy. *How to Read a City Map.* Chicago: Elk Grove Press, 1967.